God, Prayer, and Sarah Palin:
Sarah Palin and The Power of Prayer:
The Power of Prayer and Sarah Palin

By: Kristina Benson

F
910.7
.P35
B4630
2008

God, Prayer, and Sarah Palin: Sarah Palin and The Power of Prayer: The Power of Prayer and Sarah Palin

978-1-60332-062-7

Printed in the United States of America

INTRODUCTION

Christians sometimes find it difficult to determine God's will for their lives. Unlike Moses and other beneficiaries of God's voice and direct words, most of us are left to figure out God's path through far more subtle means.

In order to find God's direction, it is possible to go to church and listen to your pastor, minister, or preacher, and learn from him or her. But this must be supplemented by mindfulness on your own time. It isn't possible to learn much of anything, let alone God's will, via three hours a week on a Sunday.

This book is divided into several sections, including, among other things:

-the tradition of prayer in the Bible

-methods of prayer

-types of prayer

-strategies for incorporating prayer into your life.

Remember, if you ask humbly, you will receive.

SARAH PALIN: ONE OF US!

As a Christian, I don't need to tell you how important it is that Sarah Palin was chosen for the Vice Presidential spot on the Republican ticket. In her twenty-month tenure as the governor of Alaska, and in her service as mayor to her hometown of Wasilla, she has made many important reforms that we as Christians can look to as an example when we try to balance work, family, and God in our lives.

One of the lessons we can learn from her is the power of prayer to channel the energies of who we are and what we stand for. For example, she won her local election by a landslide, and used her business savvy to select the town's first lobbyist, sending him to Washington DC on behalf of the little town of Wasilla. Some criticized her for being too big her for britches and acting as though she was running a cosmopolitan place like New York; not a tiny town of 9,000, but Sarah had the vision to see into the future, and let her prayer guide her in achieving that vision.

The lobbyist helped Wasilla obtain federal funds (according to a story ran on September 3 2008 in the LA Times, about $1,000 per each of Wasilla's 9,000 residents) for a new park, roads, infrastructure, and library, and raised taxes to make sure that public safety and roads were always first. The $11.9 million dollars in earmarks that Wasilla received under Sarah's supervision always went to help the people, not the special interests. When Sarah faced criticism, it was often God she turned to for guidance and strength.

Sarah also wanted the hearts and minds of the people of Wasilla to be turned towards God and filled with spiritually nourishing thoughts. According to a September 4, 2008 article in the Wall Street Journal, Sarah showed her determination and dedication to the spiritual health of her townspeople by refusing to let their tax dollars fund corrupt and morally bankrupt books placed in the public library. She considered the idea of removing offensive and morally bankrupt books from the shelves of the library lest children fell prey to their influence, but was ultimately drawn to pursue bigger concerns, such as fighting corruption.

When she left her position as mayor, the town was in debt, however, with Alaska's burgeoning oil reserves, and higher taxes on oil companies to balance out the millions of dollars in debt with which they had been left, they had little to fear.

Her first order of business as governor was to create a culture of life and moral purity in the state. Not wishing to encourage an environment of promiscuity, she cut spending that went to help unmarried pregnant teens complete high school, and stated that sexual education programs that were explicit would not find her support. She advocated for teaching creation in schools, telling the Anchorage Daily News that schools should not fear teaching creationism alongside evolution. "Teach both. You know, don't be afraid of information.... Healthy debate is so important and it's so valuable in our schools. I am a proponent of teaching both. And you know, I say this too as a daughter of a science teacher." and when speaking to her church in Wasilla, asked that they pray for the troops in Iraq, as they are on a mission from God.

She fired her chef and put her plane for sale on Ebay, and encouraged the citizens of Alaska to kill the grey wolves that harass the moose populations. Always an advocate of efficiency, she championed the practice of shooting down entire packs of wolves from planes or helicopters. As an incentive, those who brought the left foreleg of a wolf were given $150. She also opposed the classification of the polar bear as an endangered species because it would make it difficult to use the resources of Alaska for the benefit of the people of the United States.

Many bloggers, including Dr. Laura Schlessinger, have criticized women with young children who choose to have a career. But Sarah is not dissuaded. She speaks openly about the role that faith plays in her life, her love of country, and her views about politics:

They will take the phrase 'under God' away from me when my cold, dead lips can no longer utter those words. God bless America.", she said in a letter to the editor.
And the pastor of her Church in Wasilla, the Bible Church, has also contributed to the shaping of her world view, as quoted in Harper's Magazine:

From an April 27, 2008 sermon: "If you really want to know where you came from and happen to believe the word of God that you are not a descendant of a chimpanzee, this is what the word of God says. I believe this version."

From a July 8, 2007 sermon: "Those that die without Christ have a horrible, horrible surprise."

From a July 28, 2007 sermon: "Do you believe we're in the last days? After listening to Newt Gingrich and the prime minister of Israel and a number of others at our gathering, I became convinced, and I have been convinced for some time. We are living in the last days. These are incredible times to live in."

Of course, as governor, she is now living in Juneau, but has found a new church that is similarly in tune with her patriotism and values. Her new pastor is similarly passionate about God and America:

From a November 25, 2007 sermon: "The purpose for the United States is... to glorify God. This nation is a Christian nation."

From an October 28, 2007 sermon: "God will not be mocked. I don't care what the ACLU says. God will not be mocked. I don't care what atheists say. God will not be mocked. I don't care what's going on in the nation today with so much horrific rebellion and sin and things that take place. God will not be mocked. Judgment Day is coming. Where do you stand?"

From an October 28, 2007 sermon: "Just giving in a little bit is a disastrous thing...You can't serve both man and God. It is one or the other."

Those of us who see ourselves in Palin can help by organizing our communities and getting the word out.

Remember the most famous community organizer of all was Jesus, and he never gave up or gave in.

To help her get elected, talk to friends about the policies she supported as governor that helped working women, and working families. Talk about what she did to protect the environment for sportswomen and sportsmen like her, so we can continue to enjoy God's bounty. And don't ever forget to pray!

PART ONE:

TRADITION

Meaning of the Tradition of Prayer

Some people devote themselves to prayer with enthusiasm, however, if asked, they don't even know the basics of what they are saying. For instance, why do we say "amen" after a prayer? Most Christians, I'm sure you will find, don't know the origin of this word, nor what it means. For instance, most don't know that the word "amen" exists both in Hebrew and in Arabic, and means "I believe."

The word Amen (is a declaration of affirmation found in the Hebrew Bible and the New Testament. It has always been in use within Judaism and Islam and later was adopted in Christian worship as a concluding formula for prayers and hymns.

The word is commonly said to be of a Hebrew origin, introduced to the West by Greek translators of the Bible. The word exists in Hebrew, Arabic, and Berber, but it has been suggested that this word as religious term may have come from the name of the Egyptian god Amun.

Three distinct Biblical usages may be noted:

1. Initial *Amen,* referring back to words of another speaker, e.g. 1 Kings 1:36; Revelation 22:20.

2. Detached *Amen,* the complementary sentence being suppressed, e.g. Nehemiah 5:13; Revelation 5:14 (cf. 1 Corinthians 14:16).

3. Final *Amen,* with no change of speaker, as in the subscription to the first three divisions of the Psalter and in the frequent doxologies of the New Testament Epistles.

Jesus used the word to affirm his own utterances, not those of another person. The liturgical use of the word in apostolic times is attested by the passage from 1 Corinthians cited above, and Justin Martyr (c. 150) describes the congregation as responding "amen," to the benediction after the celebration of the Eucharist. Among certain Gnostic sects Amen became the name of an angel.

In the King James Bible, the word amen is preserved in a number of contexts. Notable ones include:

1. The catechism of curses of the Law found in Deuteronomy 27.

2. A double *amen* ("amen and amen") occurs in Psalm 89.

3. The custom of closing prayers with *amen* originates in the Lord's Prayer at Matthew 6:13

4. *Amen* occurs in several doxology formulas in Romans 1:25, 9:5, 11:36, 15:33, and several times in Chapter 16.

5. It concludes all of Paul's general epistles.

6. In Revelation 3:14, Jesus is referred to as, "the Amen, the faithful and true witness."

7. *Amen* concludes the New Testament at Rev. 22:21.

PRAYER IN THE BIBLE

In order for God to speak to us, we need to be listening for his voice. As we spend time in prayer, we may sense God's hand in our lives. The power of prayer should not be underestimated.

The Bible, in fact, is literally filled with exhortations to pray, and pray often:

Old Testament Texts

We shall say much, and yet shall want words: but the sum of our words is, He is all. What shall we be able to do to glorify him? For the Almighty himself is above all his works. The Lord is terrible and exceeding great, and his power is admirable. Glorify the Lord as much as ever you can, for he will yet far exceed, and his magnificence is wonderful. Blessing the Lord, exalt him as much as you can: for he is above all praise. When you exalt him, put forth all your strength, and be not weary: for you can never go far enough. Eccius. 43:29-34.

You shall call upon me, and you shall go: and you shall pray to me, and I will hear you. You shall seek me, and shall find me, when you shall seek me with all your heart. <u>Jer. 29: 12-14</u>.

Cry to me, and I will hear you; and I will show you great things, and sure things which you know not. <u>Jer. 33:3</u>.

Seek the Lord and his power, seek his face evermore. And say : Save us, O God our Savior: and gather us together, and deliver us from the nations, that we may give glory to your holy name. <u>1 Paralipomenon 16:11, 35</u>. [Modern translations call this book <u>Chronicles</u>.]

Ask what you wilt that I should give you. <u>3K.3:5</u>. (<u>In the NIV 1Kings 3:5</u>)

Seek the Lord while he may be found: call upon him while he is near. <u>Is. 55:6</u>.

Let us lift up our hearts with our hands to the Lord in the heavens. <u>Lam. 3:41</u>.

Let nothing hinder you from praying always. <u>Eccius. 18:22</u>.

Pray to the Lord for the city. Jer. 29:7.

Love God all your life, and call upon him for your salvation. Ecclus. 13: 18.

Lay open your works to the Lord, and your thoughts shall be directed. Prv. 16:3 DR [Compare this with the NIV Prov. 16:3.]

Commit your way to the Lord, and trust in him, and he will do it. Ps. 36:5DR. [NIV Ps. 37:5.]

I will restore to the people a chosen lip, that all may call upon the name of the Lord, and may serve him with one shoulder. Soph. 3:9. [This book is now called Zephaniah. See this passage in the NAB and NIV.]

I will pour out upon the house of David, and upon the inhabitants of Jerusalem, the spirit of grace and of prayers. Zach. 12:10. [This prophecy refers to Christ, "whom they have pierced", who is of the house of David and his heir. We who are his followers are members of his household and part of the new Jerusalem.] Compare the NAB, and NIV.

New Testament Texts

Love your enemies: do good to them that hate you: and pray for them that persecute and <u>calumniate</u> you. <u>DR</u>, <u>Mat. 5:43-44</u> NIV, <u>NAB</u>.

The Lord's Prayer. <u>Mat. 6:7-15</u> NIV, <u>NAB</u>. (Cf. <u>Mark 11:24-25 ; Luke 11: 1-4</u>.)

Pray therefore the Lord of the harvest, that he send forth laborers into his harvest. <u>Mat. 9:38</u>.

Watch and pray that you enter not into temptation. The spirit indeed is willing, but the flesh is weak. <u>Mat. 26:41</u>.

Take heed, watch and pray. For you know not when the time is. <u>Mark 13:33</u> NASB.

Bless them that curse you and pray for them that calumniate you. <u>Luke 6:28</u>. [Calumnate is translated abuse in the NIV.]

When he was come to the place, he said to them: Pray, lest you enter into temptation. <u>Luke 22:40</u>.

I beseech you therefore, brethren, through our Lord Jesus Christ and by the charity of the Holy Ghost, that you help me in your prayers to God, that I may be delivered from the unbelievers that are in Judea and that the oblation of my service may be acceptable in Jerusalem to the saints. Rom. 15:30-31 NIV.

By all prayer and supplication praying at all times in the spirit: and in the same watching with all instance and supplication for all the saints. Eph. 6:18.

Be nothing solicitous [i.e. have no anxiety]: but in everything, by prayer and supplication, with thanksgiving, let your petitions be made known to God. Phil. 4:6.

Be instant in prayer: watching in it with thanksgiving. Praying withal for us also, that God may open unto us a door of speech to speak the mystery of Christ (for which also I am bound): that I may make it manifest as I ought to speak. Col. 4:3.

Pray for us that the word of God may run and may be glorified, even as among you: and that we may be delivered from importunate and evil men: for all men have not faith. 2 Thess. 3: 1 .

I desire therefore, first of all, that supplication, prayers, intercessions and thanksgivings be made for all men: for kings and for all that are in high station: that we may lead a quiet and a peaceable life in all piety and chastity. 1 Tim. 2: 1-3. [Piety and chastity are translated differently in the various texts. See Nasb = dignity, NIV = holiness, WEB = godliness and reverence, and especially the NAB which has devotion and dignity.]

Let us go therefore with confidence to the throne of grace: that we may obtain mercy and find grace in seasonable aid. Heb. 4:16.

If any of you want wisdom, let him ask of God who gives to all men abundantly and upbraids not. And it shall be given him. Jas. 1: 5.

Is any of you sad? Let him pray. Is he cheerful in mind? Let him sing. Jas. 5:13.

Is any man sick among you? Let him bring in the priests of the church and let them pray over him, anointing him with oil in the name of the Lord. Jas. 5: 14.

Pray one for another, that you may be saved. For the continual prayer of a just man avails much. Jas. 5:16. [In the NAB it says "fervent" instead of "continual" prayer.]

QUALITIES OF PRAYER

Old Testament Texts

Before prayer prepare your soul, and be not as a man that tempts God. Ecclus. 18:23DR. [The NAB translates it as fulfilling a vow.]

[The NAB uses the word "vow" instead of "prayer". At footnote #4, the NAB suggests the topic of 18:22-23 is not prayer as we would usually understand it but the making of a vow, an act of worship involving an animal sacrifice. The NNIV translates Sirach18:22-23 thus: "Let nothing hinder you from paying a vow promptly, and do not wait until death to be released from it. Before making a vow, prepare yourself; do not be like one who puts the Lord to the test." However, St. Francis de Sales is reported to tells us: "Pray for your prayer's success."]

You have hardened your heart, and have spread your hands to him. If you will put away from yourself the iniquity that is in your hand, let not injustice remain in your tabernacle: then may you lift up your face without spot, and you shall be steadfast and shall not fear. Job 11: 13-15.

He that turns away his ears from hearing the law, his prayer shall be an abomination. Prov. 28:9.

He that adores God with joy shall be accepted, and his prayer shall approach even to the clouds. Ecclus. 35:20. NAB Sirach 35:17.

If I have looked at iniquity in my heart, the Lord will not hear me. Ps. 65:18DR. [NIV Ps 66:18.]

Think of the Lord in goodness, and seek him in simplicity of heart: for he is found by them who tempt him not: and he shows himself to them that have faith in him. Wis. 1:1DR f; NAB.

Nor from the beginning have the proud been acceptable to you: but the prayer of the humble and the meek has always pleased you. Judith. 9:16. [This verse seems to be missing from newer translations, but see Judith 9:11NAB, cf. Sir. 35:17.] [Vines: "Described negatively, meekness is the opposite to self-assertiveness and self-interest..."]

The prayer of him that humbles himself shall pierce the clouds: and until it come nigh he will not be comforted: and he will not depart till the Most High behold. Eccius. 35:21DR.

Then shall they call upon me, and I will not hear: they shall rise in the morning and shall not find me: because they have hated instruction, and received not the fear of the Lord. Prov. 1:28 -29.

He that stops his ear against the cry of the poor shall also cry himself, and shall not be heard. Prov. 21:13.

He that turns away his ears from hearing the law, his prayer shall be an abomination. Prov. 28:9.

Then this wicked man [Antiochus] prayed to the Lord, of whom he was not to obtain mercy. 2 Mac. 9: 13. NAB. ["2Macc. 9:13 Then the abominable fellow made a vow to the Lord, who would no longer have mercy on him,.." NRSV.]

You shall cry out in that day from the face of the king whom you have chosen to yourselves: and the Lord will not hear you in that day, because you desired unto yourselves a king. lKings 8:18. [In modern translations this is 1Sam. 8:18.]

Then shall they cry to the Lord, and he will not hear them: and he will hide his face from them at that time, as they have behaved wickedly in their devices. Mich. 3:4 DR, NAB.

The prayer of the humble and the meek have always
pleased you, O God of the heavens, Creator of the waters,
and Lord of the whole creation, hear me a poor wretch
making supplication to you and presuming on your mercy.
Judith. 9: 16. [Modern translations apparently omit this
verse.]

New Testament Texts

When you pray, you shall not be as the hypocrites that love
to stand and pray in the synagogues and corners of the
streets, that they may be seen by men. Amen I say to you,
they have received their reward. But when you shall pray,
enter into your chamber The Lord is far from the wicked,
and, having shut the door, pray to your and he will hear the
prayers of the Father in secret: and your Father who sees in
secret will repay you. Mat. 6:5-6.

When you are praying, speak not much, as the heathens.
For they think that in their much speaking they may be
heard. Mat. 6:7.

This people honors me with their lips: but their heart is far from me. Mat. 15:8.

Woe to you scribes and Pharisees, hypocrites, because you devour the houses of widows, praying long prayers. Mat. 23: 14 [NASB].

When you shall stand to pray, forgive, if you have anything against any man: that your Father also, who is in heaven, may forgive you your sins. Mark 11:25.

Parable of the Pharisee and the publican. Luke 18:10-14.

God is a spirit: and they that adore him must adore him in spirit and in truth. John 4:24.

The Spirit also helps our infirmity. For we know not what we should pray for as we ought: but the Spirit himself asks for us with unspeakable groanings. Rom. 8:26.

I will pray with the spirit, I will pray also with the understanding. 1 Cor. 14:15 DR. [Compare 1Cor. 14:15 NIV and NAB.]

Let him ask in faith, nothing wavering. Jas. 1:6.

You ask and receive not: because you ask amiss. <u>Jas. 4:3</u>.

This is the confidence which we have towards him: that, whatsoever we shall ask according to his will, he hears us. And we know that he hears whatsoever we ask: we know that we have the petitions which we request of him. <u>1 John 5:14 -15</u>.

Parable of the <u>importunate</u> friend. <u>Luke 11:5-8</u>.

Parable of the unjust judge. <u>Luke 18:1-8</u>.

EFFICACY OF PRAYER

Old Testament Texts

The lord is far from the wicked, and he will hear the prayers of the just. Prov. 15: 29.

He will do the will of them that fear him: and he will hear their prayer. Ps. 144: 19. [NIV Ps. 145:19.]

In you, O Lord, have I hoped: you wilt hear me, O Lord my God. Ps. 37:16. [Compare NIV Ps. 38:15.]

Then Eliachim the high priest of the Lord went about all Israel and spoke to them, Saying: Know you that the Lord will hear your prayers, if you continue with perseverance in fastings and prayers in the sight of the Lord. Judith. 4:10-11. [Comepare the NAB.]

Call upon me in the day of trouble. I will deliver you, and you shall glorify me. Ps. 49: 15. [NIV Ps 50:15.]

Cry to me, and I will hear you: and I will show you great things, and sure things which you knows not. Jer. 33:3.

Weeping you shall not weep. He will surely have pity on you at the voice of your cry: as soon as he shall hear, he will answer you. Is. 30: 19.

It shall come to pass that before they call I will hear: as they are yet speaking I will hear. Is. 65:24.

Neither is there any other nation so great, that have gods so nigh them, as our God is present to all our petitions. Deut. 4:7.

Who have continued in his commandment, and have been forsaken? or who have called upon him, and he despised him? Ecclus. 2:12.

My people, being converted, shall make supplication to me, and seek out my face, and do penance from their most wicked ways: then I will hear from heaven, and will forgive their sins, and will heal their land. 2 Par. 7:14.

New Testament Texts

Ask, and it shall be given you, seek, and you shall find: knock, and it shall be opened to you. Mat. 7:7. NAB.

If you then being evil, know how to give good gifts to your children: how much more will your Father who is in heaven give good things to them that ask him? Mat. 7:11. NAB

If two of you shall consent upon earth concerning anything whatsoever they shall ask, it shall be done to them by my Father who is in heaven. Mat. 18:19. NAB.

All things whatsoever you shall ask in prayer believing, you shall receive. Mat. 21:22. NAB.

When he was come into the house, his disciples secretly asked him: Why could not we cast him out? And he said to them: This kind can go out by nothing, but by prayer and fasting. Mark 9:27-28. [The NIV and other translations drop the word "fasting" which is not in all manuscripts. See the NASB. Also the instances in the NIV where fasting and prayer are mentioned.]

All things, whatsoever you ask when you pray, believe that you shall receive: and they shall come unto you. Mark 11:24. NAB.

Fear not, Zachary, for your prayer is heard. Luke 1:13. NAB

We know that God does not hear sinners: but if a man be a server of God and does his will, him he hears. John 9:31. NAB.

Whatsoever you shall ask the Father in my name, that will I do: that the Father may be glorified in the Son. If you shall ask me anything in my name, that I will do. John 14: 13 f. NAB.

If you abide in me and my words abide in you, you shall ask whatever you will: and it shall be done unto you. John 15:7. NAB.

In that day you shall not ask me anything. Amen, amen I say to you: if you ask the Father anything in my name, he will give it you. Hitherto you have not asked anything in my name. Ask, and you shall receive: that your joy may be full. John 16:23 -24.

Whosoever shall call upon the name of the Lord shall be saved. Rom. 10:13. NAB.

Let him bring in the priests of the church and let them pray over him, anointing him with oil in the name of the Lord. And the prayer of faith shall save the sick man. And the Lord shall raise him up: and if he be in sins, they shall be forgiven him. Jas. 5: 15. NAB.

Pray one for another, that you may be saved. For the continual prayer of a just man avails much. Jas. 5:16. NAB.

If our heart do not reprehend us, we have confidence towards God. And whatsoever we shall ask, we shall receive of him: because we keep his commandments and do those things which are pleasing in his sight. 1 John 3:21 -22.

This is the confidence which we have towards him: that, whatsoever we shall ask according to his will, he hears us. 1 John 5:14.

TIMES OF PRAYER

Old Testament Texts

We ought to prevent the sun to bless you, and adore you at the dawning of the light. Wis. 16:28DR. [Compare he NAB: "So that men might know that one must give you thanks before the sunrise, and turn to you at daybreak. "]

In the morning I will stand before you, and will see, because you art not a God that wills iniquity. Ps. 5:5. [See NIV Ps. 5:3-4.]

Arise, give praise in the night; in the beginning of the watches pour out your heart like water before the face of the Lord. Lam. 2:19.

O God, my God, to you do I watch at break of day. For you my soul has thirsted; for you my flesh, O how many ways! Ps. 62:1 [NIV Ps. 63:1].

If I have remembered you upon my bed, I will meditate on you in the morning, because you have been my helper. Ps. 62:7 [NIV Ps. 63:7].

I rose at midnight to give praise to you, for the judgments of your justification. Ps. 118:62. [Psalm 119:62 in the NAB: "At midnight I rise to praise you because your edicts are just."]

Seven times a day I have given praise to you, for the judgments of your justice. Ps. 118: 164. [Psalm 119:164 in NAB: "Seven times a day I praise you because your edicts are just. "]

When Daniel knew this, that is to say, that the law was made, he went Into his house: and opening the window in his upper chamber towards Jerusalem, he knelt down three times a day, and adored, and gave thanks before his God, as he had been accustomed to do before. Dan. 6: 10. [See NAB at verse 11.]

Let tears run down like a torrent day and night: give thyself no rest, and let not the apple of your eye cease. Arise, give praise in the night, in the beginning of the watches: pour out your heart like water before the face of the Lard, lift up your hands to him. Lam. 2:18f. NAB.

New Testament Texts

Watch, therefore, praying at all times. Luke 21:36.

Peter and John went up into the temple at the ninth hour of prayer. Acts 3:1.

Peter went up to the highest parts of the house to pray about the sixth hour. Acts 10:9.

At midnight, Paul and Silas praying, praised God. And they that were in prison heard them. Acts 16:25.

When he had said these things, kneeling down, he prayed with them all. And there was much weeping among them all. And falling on the neck of Paul, they kissed him, being grieved most of all for the word which he had said, that they should see his face no more. And they brought him on his way to the ship. Acts 20:36-38.

Take unto you the helmet of salvation and the sword of the Spirit (which is the word of God). By all prayer and supplication praying at all times in the spirit: and in the same watching with all instance and supplication for all the saints. Eph. 6: 17-18.

PLACES OF PRAYER

Old Testament Texts

That you may hearken to the prayer, which your servant prays in this place to you [i.e. God's house]. 3 K. 8:29. NAB.

If heaven shall be shut up, and there shall be no rain, because of their sins, and they, praying in this place, shall do penance to your name and shall be converted from their sins, by occasion of their affliction: then hear you them in heaven. 3 K. 8:35 f. NAB.

That you may open your eyes upon this house, day and night, upon the place wherein you have promised that your name should be called upon, and that you would hear the prayer which your servant prays in it... Whosoever shall pray in this place, hear you from your dwelling place, that is, from heaven. 2 Par. 6:20 f.

But yet the people sacrificed in the high places: for there was no temple built to the name of the Lord until that day. 3K.3:2. [In the NIV this is 1 Kings 3:2.]

New Testament Texts

[When you] pray, enter into your chamber and, having shut the door, pray to your Father in secret: and your Father who sees in secret will repay you. Mat. 6:6.

It is written: My house shall be called the house of prayer. Mat. 21:13.

Our fathers adored on this mountain: and you say that at Jerusalem Is the place where men must adore. Jesus said to her: Woman, believe me that the hour is coming, when you shall neither on this mountain nor in Jerusalem adore the Father. John 4:20-24.

All these were persevering with one mind in prayer, with the women and Mary the mother of Jesus, and with his brethren. Acts 1: 14.

Continuing daily with one accord in the temple and breaking bread from house to house, they took their meat with gladness and simplicity of heart, praising God. Acts 2:46 f.

Upon the Sabbath day, we went forth without the gate by a river side, where it seemed that there was prayer. <u>Acts 16: 13</u>.

Departing we went forward, they all bringing us on our way, with their wives and children, till we were out of the city. And we kneeled down on the shore: and we prayed. <u>Acts 21:5</u>.

I will therefore that men pray in every place, lifting up pure hands, without anger and contention. <u>1 Tim. 2:8</u>.

EXAMPLES OF PRAYER

By Christ

Having dismissed the multitudes, he went into a mountain alone to pray. Matt. 14:23

Rising very early, going out, he went Into a desert place: and there he prayed. Mark 1: 35.

When he had dismissed them, he went up to the mountain to pray. Mark 6:46.

It came to pass, when all the people were baptized, that Jesus also being baptized and praying, heaven was opened. Luke 3:21.

He retired into the desert and prayed. Luke 5:l6.

He went out into a mountain to pray: and he passed the whole night in the prayer of God. Luke 6: 12.

It came to pass, as he was alone praying, his disciples also were with him: and he asked them, saying: Whom do the people say that I am? Luke 9: 18.

It came to pass, about eight days after these words, that he took Peter and James and John and went up into a mountain to pray. And while he prayed, the shape of his countenance was altered and his raiment became white and glittering. Luke 9:28 f.

As he was in a certain place praying, when he ceased, one of his disciples said to him: Lord, teach us to pray, as John also taught his disciples. And he said to them: When you pray, say: Father, hallowed be your name. Luke 11:1 -4.

I have prayed for you, that your faith fail not: and you, being once converted, confirm your brethren. Luke 22:32. NAB.

Going a little further, he fell upon his face, praying and saying: My Father, if It be possible, let this chalice pass from me. Nevertheless, not as I will but as you will. . . . Again the second time, he went and prayed, saying: My Father, if this chalice may not pass, but I must drink it, your will be done. And he came again and found them sleeping: for their eyes were heavy. And leaving them, he went again: and he prayed the third time, saying the selfsame word. Mat. 26:39, 42-44.

Jesus said: Father, forgive them, for they know not what they do. Luke 23:34.

Jesus crying with a loud voice, said: Father, into your hands I commend my spirit. Luke 23:46.

Jesus lifting up his eyes, said: Father, I give you thanks that you have heard me. And I knew that you hear me always; but because of the people who stand about have I said it, that they may believe that you have sent me. When he had said these things, he cried with a loud voice: Lazarus, come forth. John 11:41-43.

Christ's prayer after the Last Supper. John 17:1-26.

Prayer to Christ

A leper came and adored him, saying: Lord, if you wilt, you can make me clean. And Jesus stretching forth his hand, touched him, saying: I will. Be you made clean. And forthwith his leprosy was cleansed. Mat. 8:2 f.

A great tempest arose in the sea, so that the boat was covered with waves, but he was asleep. And they came to him and awaked him, saying: Lord, save us, we perish. Mat. 8:24 ff. NAB.

As Jesus passed from thence, there followed him two blind men crying out and saying: Have mercy on us,O Son of David. Mat. 9:27. NAB.

Peter making answer, said: Lord, if It be you, bid me to come to you upon the waters. And he said: Come. And Peter going down out of the boat walked upon the water to come to Jesus. But seeing the wind strong, he was afraid: and when he began to sink, he cried out, saying: Lord, save me. Mat. 14:28-30.

Behold a woman of Canaan, who came out of those coasts, crying out, said to him: Have mercy on me, O Lord, you Son of David: my daughter is grievously troubled by a devil. Mat. 15:22. NAB.

Two blind men sitting by the wayside heard that Jesus passed by. And they cried out, saying: O Lord, you Son of David, have mercy on us. And Jesus stood and called them and said: What will ye that I do to you? They say to him:

Lord, that our eyes be opened. And Jesus having compassion on them, touched their eyes. And immediately they saw and followed him. Mat. 20:30-34.

They bring to him one deaf and dumb: and they besought him that he would lay his hand upon him. Mark 7:32. NAB.

They came to Bethsalda: and they bring to him a blind man. And they besought him that he would touch him. Mark 8:22. NAB.

One of the multitude, answering, said: Master, I have brought my son to you, having a dumb spirit. Oftentimes he has cast him into the fire and into the waters to destroy him. But if you can do anything, help us, having compassion on us. And Jesus said to him: If you can believe, all things are possible to him that believes. And immediately the father of the boy crying out, with tears said: I do believe, Lord. Help my unbelief. Mark 9: 16, 21-23.

Jesus answering, said to him: What wilt you that I should do to you? And the blind man said. to him: Rabboni, that I may see. Mark 10:51. NAB.

Jesus rising up out of the synagogue, went into Simon's house. And Simon's wife's mother was taken with a great fever: and they besought him for her. And standing over her, he commanded the fever: and it left her. Luke 4:38-40. NAB.

As he entered into a certain town, there met him ten men that were lepers, who stood afar off and lifted up their voice, saying: Jesus, Master, have mercy on us. Luke 17:12 f. NAB.

He said to Jesus: Lord, remember me when you shall come into your kingdom. And Jesus said to him. Amen I say to you: This day you shall be with me in paradise. Luke 23:42 f. NAB.

He having heard that Jesus was come from Judea into Galilee, went to him and prayed him to come down and heal his son: for he was at the point of death. Jesus therefore said to him: Unless you see signs and wonders you believe not. The ruler saith to him: Lord come down before that my son die. John 4:47-49.NAB.

When he had entered into Capharnaum there came to him a centurion beseeching him and saying: Lord my servant is grievously tormented. And Jesus saith to him: I will come and heal him. Mat. 8:5-7. NAB.

OTHER PRAYERS

Old Testament Texts

When thou didst pray with tears, and didst bury the dead, and didst leave thy dinner, and hide the dead by day In thy house, and bury them by night, I offered thy prayer to the Lord. And now the Lord hath sent me to heal thee, and to deliver Sara thy son's wife from the devil. Tob. 12: 12, 14.

Isaac besought the Lord for his wife, because she was barren: and he heard him, and made Rebecca to conceive. Gen. 25:21. NIV

When the Jews heard of Nicanor's coming, and that the nations were assembled against them, they cast earth upon their heads, and made supplication to him, who chose his people, to keep them forever, and who protected his portion by evident signs. 2 Mac. 14:15.

Judas and they that were with him, encountered them, calling upon God by prayers. So fighting with their hands, but praying to the Lord with their hearts, they slew no less than five and thirty thousand, being greatly cheered with the presence of God. 2 Mac. 15:26-27.

Blot out, O Lord, my iniquities as a cloud, and as a mist my sins. Is. 44:22.

Have mercy on us, O Lord, and put away our iniquities, and cast all our sins into the bottom of the sea. Mich. 7:19. NIV. cf NAB.

See my abjection and my labor: and forgive me all my sins. Ps. 24:18. [NIV Ps. 25:18.]

If thou, O Lord, wilt mark iniquities; Lord, who shall stand it? Ps. 129:3. [NIV 130:3.]

Turn to me, O Lord, and deliver my soul: o save me for thy mercy's sake. Ps.6:5. [In the NIV see Ps. 6:2-5.]

O forgive me, that I may be refreshed before I go hence and be no more. Ps. 38: 14. In NAB psalm 39.

Evils without number have surrounded me; my iniquities have overtaken me, and I was not able to see. They are multiplied above the hairs of my head; and my heart hath forsaken me. Be pleased, O Lord, to deliver me: look down, O Lord, to help me. Ps. 39:13 f. [NIV Ps. 40:12-13.]

Heal me, O Lord, and I shall be healed: save me, and I shall be saved. Jer. 17:14.

And now, O Lord, thou art our Father, and we are clay: and thou art our Maker, and we all are the works of thy hands. Be not very angry, O Lord, and remember no longer our iniquity: behold, see we are all thy people. Is. 64:8 f. NAB.

In the multitude of thy mercy hear me. Draw me out of the mire, that I may not stick fast: deliver me from them that hate me, and out of the deep waters. Let not the tempest of water drown me, nor the deep swallow me up: and let not the pit shut her mouth upon me. Ps. 68:14-16. [In the NIV see Ps. 69:13-16.]

Bow down thy ear to me: make haste to deliver me. Be thou unto me a God, a protector, and a house of refuge to save me. Ps. 30:3. [In the NIV see Ps. 31:2.]

Turn not away thy face from me: in the day when I am in trouble, incline thy ear to me. In what day soever I shall call upon thee, hear me speedily. Ps. 101:3. [In the NIV 102:2.]

Hear us, O God our Savior, who art the hope of all the ends of the earth, and in the sea afar off. Ps. 64:6. [NIV 65:4-5.]

Prayer of Jabez "Jabez was the most distinguished of the brothers. His mother had named him Jabez, saying, "I bore him with pain." Jabez prayed to the God of Israel: "Oh, that you may truly bless me and extend my boundaries! Help me and make me free of misfortune, without pain!" And God granted his prayer." 1Chronicles 4:9-10 NAB or 1 Paralipomenon 4:9-10 in the Douay, and NIV.

New Testament Texts

She was a widow until fourscore and four years: who departed not from the temple, by fastings and prayers serving night and day. Luke 2:37. NAB.

They said to him: Why do the disciples of John fast often and make prayers, and the disciples of the Pharisees in like manner: but thine eat and drink? Luke 5:33. NAB.

All these were persevering with one mind in prayer, with the women and Mary the mother of Jesus, and with his brethren. Acts 1: 14. NAB.

And they were persevering in the doctrine of the apostles and in the communication of the breaking of bread and in prayers. Acts 2:42. NAB. [The breaking of bread means the Eucharist, the mass, in primitive form. See Acts 2:42 footnote #8. See generally, Eucharist: Breading Bread.]

When they had prayed, the place was moved wherein they were assembled: and they were all filled with the Holy Ghost. Acts 4:31. NAB.

This man saw in a vision manifestly, about the ninth hour of the day, an angel of God coming in unto him and saying to him: Cornelius. And he, beholding him, being seized with fear, said: What is it, Lord? And he said to him: Thy prayers and thy alms are ascended for a memorial in the sight of God. Acts 10:3 f. NAB.

Peter therefore was kept in prison. But prayer was made without ceasing by the church unto God for him. Acts 12:5. NAB.

When they had ordained to them <u>priests</u> in every church and had prayed with fasting, they commended them to the Lord, in whom they believed. Acts 14:22. <u>NAB.</u> [The New American Bible gives *presbyter* insead of *priest*. This office involves more than the general priesthood of the faithful. See <u>footnote 5</u>.]

The father of Publius lay sick of a fever and of a bloody <u>flux</u>. To whom Paul entered in: and when he had prayed and laid his hands on him, he healed him. <u>Acts 28:8</u>.

God is my witness, whom I serve in my spirit in the gospel of his Son, that without ceasing I make a commemoration of you: always in my prayers making request, if by any means now at length I may have a prosperous journey, by the will of God, to come unto you. <u>Rom. 1:9 -10</u>.

Wherefore, I also, hearing of your faith that is in the Lord Jesus and of your love towards all the saints, cease not to give thanks for you, making commemoration of you in my prayers. <u>Eph. 1:15 ff</u>.

I give thanks to my God in every remembrance of you: always in all my prayers making supplication for you all with joy. <u>Phil. 1:3-5</u>.

Therefore we also, from the day that we heard it, cease not to pray for you and to beg that you may be filled with the knowledge of his 'will. in all wisdom and spiritual understanding. Col. 1:9-12.

Epaphras saluteth you, who Is one of you, a servant of Christ Jesus, who is always solicitous for you in prayer., that you may stand perfect and full In all the will of God. Col. 4:12. NAB.

We give thanks to God always for you all: making a remembrance of you in our prayers without ceasing. 1 Thess. 1:2. NAB.

We pray always for you: that our God would make you worthy of his vocation and fulfil all the good pleasure of his goodness and the work of faith in power: that the name of our Lord Jesus may be glorified in you, and you in him, according to the grace of the Lord Jesus Christ. 2 Thess. 1:11-12.

I give thanks to God, whom I serve from my forefathers, with a pure conscience, that without ceasing I have a remembrance of thee in my prayers night and day. 2 Tim. 1:3. NAB.

Concerning all things, I make it my prayer that thou mayest proceed prosperously and fare well as thy soul doth prosperously. 3 John 2.

I give thanks to my God, always making a remembrance of thee in my prayers. Philem. 4.

The Magnificat. Luke 1:46-56.

The Benedictus. Luke 1:68-79.

HOW TO PRAY

Most of us were introduced to prayer at a young age. I vividly remember kneeling beside my bed, hands clasped, chanting:

> Now I lay me down to sleep
> I pray the Lord my soul to keep
> And if I die before I wake
> I pray the Lord my soul to take.

I said the words dutifully as I grew up, but I never knew exactly what they meant, or why I was supposed to say them. As I got older, I began to wonder exactly what else I should be doing when praying.

Few of us, I believe, were introduced to the idea of silent prayer, being silent in God's presence, or an individual relationship with God.

Prayer doesn't necessarily have to be an activity that takes place in silence, on your knees, hands clasped. It can be any activity that cultivates our relationship with God, no matter how mundane. If reading the Bible brings you closer to God, that is prayer. Working in a garden, running along the beach, visiting a national park, studying the world He created, doing charitable works...all can become prayer.

The caveat, however, is that something you enjoy can't necessarily be a meaningful prayer unless it is conducted with mindfulness. You could go jogging because you ate a cupcake and want to work off the extra calories. Or you could go because you want to be in His beauty and experience the gifts of His bounty. You could read Scripture mindlessly in a hotel room to pass the time, or in church if not particularly enthralled with the sermon. Or you could read with a focused desire to learn and understand God's words.

Mindfulness, then, is the degree to which we invest our hearts and souls into any activity. It is being fully present to God in the moment. Cooking a meal with our hearts centered on God is more of a prayer than the sitting in church, mind wandering, while looking forward to what we can move on to when it is over.

The following questions might help you develop a better sense of what prayer means to you, and how to nurture your relationship with God.

- How do **you** pray?

- In what settings do you pray?

- What do you pray for? Do you receive it? Do you receive something else? What do you feel when you do not receive it?

- When you pray, what thoughts most often break in? Do they spring from the prayer, or do they take you away from the prayer?

- When have you found yourself losing the sense of God's presence in prayer? Have you found out why? What was the lesson you learned, if any?

- Have you ever been so concerned about someone that you felt **driven** to pray for them?

- How and why does your church pray? How often do they meet for it?

- Does your church have any goals for their prayer life? How can these goals be gauged or measured?

- How embarrassed do you get when praying aloud in the presence of others? Do you pray for different things when praying with them than in private?

- Some groups take on a special burden or concern in prayer, like, say, a nation, a missionary, a neighborhood, those struck with a certain disease, etc. What similar concern most touches the heart of you or those praying with you?

- How can the group's/church's prayers best support its purposes?

- What was the most intense prayer that your group ever prayed? What do you think caused that level of intensity?

- Within the service, when do the worshippers pray? When does the priest or leader pray?

- What do they pray for? Why do you think they pray for that within a worship service?

- In what ways are the prayers a part of what binds the worshippers together? What is it that they are praying for in it?

- What do you think such prayer does for those praying it?

- For those being prayed about?

- What do you notice about what they are praying about, and how they are praying about it?

- Do you find any of it disturbing? Why?

- Which of these Psalms do you connect most with? Why? What do you *expect* from prayer?

- Have you ever received it? Did the Divine response surprise you?

- When have you most felt that you had lost touch with God?

- When have you felt most intimate with God?

- How have these moments affected your prayers?

- Have you ever been angry *at God*? If so, when did you *tell* that to God? Did there seem to be a response, then or later?

- Have you ever felt afraid to pray? Why?

- Does anyone else you know seem to fear something about prayer?

- What do you think God *really* thinks of you?

- When have you prayed for something, when you look back on it, you're glad you didn't get?

- Or prayed that it would not happen, but you're glad it did? How would your life be different if God had granted those prayers?

- How do you think you'd feel if God woke you up out of a sound sleep? If you've experienced this yourself, what did you do next?

- When you ask God to forgive you, do you *accept* that forgiveness?

- What have you been *afraid* to ask God? Why?

- When you were ill or in serious trouble, did you ever *feel* the prayers of others? What was that like?

- What were you getting from those prayers?

- What other effects did the prayers have?

-Was there ever anything that you felt was personally demeaning or insulting to put before God in prayer? Why?

- About the gifted prayer folks around you: what do you think makes their intercessions special?

- What is the strangest prayer you ever heard someone pray?

- What do you most remember from your childhood about prayer?

    *How were you taught to pray? As you look back on it, can you identify what you enjoyed about prayer?

    *is there anything that may have been missing from your early experiences with prayer?

* Make a list of all the things you do that nurtures your relationship with God if performed mindfully and fully present in His glory.

* What activities could you turn into prayer if you committed to mindfulness?

* Can you imagine how your life would change if you were more intentional about prayer and paid more attention to God?

*In what way would you, your family, and your loved one benefit from a better relationship with God?

*what kinds of events or occurrences tend to distract you from prayer?

CHALLENGES IN PRAYER

It is as easy to come up with excuses to avoid praying as it is to avoid good diet and exercise.

Are you guilty of these common excuses?

> *I don't know how to pray

> *I don't have time

> *I have too much to do

> *I am not sure what to pray for

The challenges that stand in the way of our prayer can, in fact, be overcome with prayer itself.

If we try to figure out who God is before we pray, we may never pray. God is a mystery that is incomprehensible to mere mortals. Similarly, if we wait to pray until we have the right words, until we build our self-esteem, until we overcome our fear of vulnerability, we may never pray. The longer we wait to pray the more we leave God out of our lives, and out of our souls.

73

EFFECTIVENESS OF PRAYER

Often, the power of prayer has been questioned by secularists and scientists. Although most of us, who possess the belief that prayer can and does work, do not require physical, quantitative proof of the power of prayer, it is interesting to read the results of these studies.

One of the most quoted scientific studies of prayer was done between August of 1982 and May of 1983. 393 patients in the San Francisco General Hospital's Coronary Care Unit participated in a double blind study to assess the effects of intercessory prayer. Patients were randomly selected to either receive or not receive intercessory prayer. All participants in the study, including patients, doctors, and the conductor of the study himself remained blind throughout the study, To guard against biasing the study, the patients were not contacted again after it was decided which group would be prayed for, and which group would not.

It was assumed that although the patients in the control group would not be prayed for by the participants in the study, that others-family members, friends etc., would likely pray for the health of at least some of the members of the control group. Unfortunately, there was no control over this factor. Meanwhile all of the members of the group that received prayer would be prayed for by not only those associated with the study, but by others as well.

The patients who had received prayer as a part of the study were healthier and recovered faster than those who had not.

The August 31, 1998 issue of *Jet Magazine* questioned whether prayer could lower blood pressure, reporting on a study conducted by Duke University Medical Center in Durham, NC. This study had over 4,000 participants over the age of 65. The study found that those who pray and attend Christian religious services on a weekly basis, especially those between the ages of 65 and 74, had lower blood pressure than their counterparts who did not pray or attend religious services. They found that the more religious the person, particularly those who prayed or studied the Bible weekly, the lower the blood pressure. According to the study these people were forty percent less likely to have high diastolic pressure or diastolic hypertension than these were who did not attend religious services, pray, or participate in independent spiritual practices.

Though the faithful will always believe that there need not be any physical evidence of the power and effects of prayer, science has come a long way toward showing just that-prayer is real, and it works.

TYPES OF PRAYER

Prayers of Thanksgiving and Praise

Prayers of praise and thanksgiving are one of the most common forms of prayer. Prayers of gratitude are a common response to the beauty of God's creation. "Thanks be to God!" or "God bless you" are both often uttered and are a form of thanksgiving for His kindness and good works.

A simple children's prayer goes like this:

> Thank you God for all that grows,
> Thank you for the sky's rainbows,
> Thank you for the stars that shine,
> Thank you for these friends of mine,
> Thank you for the moon and sun,
> T hank you God for all you've done!
> A Thanksgiving Day prayer, by Brian F. King, says:
> O Lord, with humble hearts we pray
> Thy blessing this Thanksgiving Day
> And ask that at table place,
> Where grateful folk say words of grace,
> That Thou will come to share the yield
> Thy bounty gave to farm and field.
> We pray thy love will bless, O Lord,
> Each hearth, each home, each festive board;

And that Thy peace will come to stay
Where candles glow, Thanksgiving Day.

Or here is another example from a popular hymn:

Prayer of Praise and Thanks

Blessed are you, Lord God:
Blessed are you for ever.
Holy is your name:
Blessed are you for ever.
Great is your mercy for your people:
Blessed are you for ever.

Amen!

Father, Son, and Holy Spirit,
We praise you and give you glory:
We bless you for calling us to be your holy people.

Remain in our hearts,
And guide us in our love and service.
Help us to let our light shine before others
And lead them to the way of faith.

Holy Trinity of love,
We praise you now and for ever.

Amen!

We praise you, Father of all;
We thank you for calling us to be your people,
And for choosing us to give you glory.
In a special way we thank you for...

[State your intention here.]

Cleanse our hearts and our lives
With your holy word
And make our prayer pleasing to you.
Guide us by your Spirit
As we follow in the paths of Jesus our brother.

All glory and praise are yours, Father,
For ever and ever.

Amen!

Let us give glory to the Father
Through the Son
In the Holy Spirit,
For God has made us his people, his Church,
And calls us to sing his praises.

All honour and glory and thanks are his,
And praise and worship belong to him.
To God be glory in his Church

For ever and ever!

Amen!

Thanks for a beautiful day: On a beautiful day,
we may thank God and praise him for his many gifts.

Father of Jesus,
We praise you and give you glory
For the wonderful things you do for us;
For life and health,
for friends and family,
for this splendid day.

If in doubt, a simple hymnal can be a very inspirational source of prayer. Or you may, of course, create your own prayer of thanks.

Prayers of Anger and Sorrow

Sometimes in the experience of deep grief and anger, God seems very far away. We may feel that God has abandoned us. These are some of the most difficult times to pray, but they are probably the most necessary.

The Psalms provide guidance for this form of prayer and teach us to turn to God in our hours and days of darkness. There are also plenty of other examples of people who turned to God during their darkest hours, and found their souls soothed.

Psalm 10

10:1 Why do you stand far off, Yahweh?

Why do you hide yourself in times of trouble?

10:2 In arrogance, the wicked hunt down the weak.

They are caught in the schemes that they devise.

10:3 For the wicked boasts of his heart's cravings.

He blesses the greedy, and condemns Yahweh.

10:4 The wicked, in the pride of his face,

has no room in his thoughts for God.

10:5 His ways are prosperous at all times.

He is haughty, and your laws are far from his sight.

As for all his adversaries, he sneers at them.

10:6 He says in his heart, "I shall not be shaken.

For generations I shall have no trouble."

10:7 His mouth is full of cursing, deceit, and oppression.

Under his tongue is mischief and iniquity.

10:8 He lies in wait near the villages.

From ambushes, he murders the innocent.

His eyes are secretly set against the helpless.

10:9 He lurks in secret as a lion in his ambush.

He lies in wait to catch the helpless.

He catches the helpless, when he draws him in his net.

10:10 The helpless are crushed.

They collapse.

They fall under his strength.

10:11 He says in his heart, "God has forgotten.

He hides his face.

He will never see it."

10:12 Arise, Yahweh!

God, lift up your hand!

Don't forget the helpless.

10:13 Why does the wicked person condemn God,

and say in his heart, "God won't call me into account?"

10:14 But you do see trouble and grief.

You consider it to take it into your hand.

You help the victim and the fatherless.

10:15 Break the arm of the wicked.

As for the evil man, seek out his wickedness until you find

none.

10:16 Yahweh is King forever and ever!

The nations will perish out of his land.

10:17 Yahweh, you have heard the desire of the humble.

You will prepare their heart.

You will cause your ear to hear,

10:18 to judge the fatherless and the oppressed,

that man who is of the earth may terrify no more.

Psalm 13

For the Chief Musician. A Psalm by David.

13:1 How long, Yahweh?
Will you forget me forever?
How long will you hide your face from me?
13:2 How long shall I take counsel in my soul,
having sorrow in my heart every day?
How long shall my enemy triumph over me?
13:3 Behold, and answer me, Yahweh, my God.
Give light to my eyes, lest I sleep in death;
13:4 Lest my enemy say, "I have prevailed against him;"
Lest my adversaries rejoice when I fall.

13:5 But I trust in your loving kindness.
My heart rejoices in your salvation.
13:6 I will sing to Yahweh,
because he has been good to me.

Psalm 43

1: Judge me, O God, and plead my cause against an ungodly nation: O deliver me from the deceitful and unjust man.

2: For thou art the God of my strength: why dost thou cast me off? why go I mourning because of the oppression of the enemy?

3: O send out thy light and thy truth: let them lead me; let them bring me unto thy holy hill, and to thy tabernacles.

4: Then will I go unto the altar of God, unto God my exceeding joy: yea, upon the harp will I praise thee, O God my God.

5: Why art thou cast down, O my soul? and why art thou disquieted within me? hope in God: for I shall yet praise him, who is the health of my countenance, and my God.

Give us this day our daily bread, O Father in heaven, and grant that we who are filled with good things from Your open hand, may never close our hearts to the hungry, the homeless, and the poor; in the name of the Father, and of the Sone, and of the Holy Spirit.

- from the abbey of New Clairvaux, Viña, California

Thanksgiving: Mirror Unto The Soul of a Nation

"A nation divided cannot stand," said Abraham Lincoln, paraphrasing Scripture. But with a bit of luck, some ordinary patience and understanding, and a touch of grace, it can. Here's how.

Thanksgiving: To Whom, For What?

A day of prayer, self-congratulations, or what? When the act of counting one's blessings becomes the habit of counting upon one's blessings. And what the holiday really means.

The Essence of Thanksgiving

A visitor to America from outer space in late November might conclude that we worship the turkey goddess. So what is the deeper meaning of this holiday, with its sometimes conflicting themes?

More Thanksgiving Prayers

Thanksgiving Thoughts and Quotations

Though our mouths were full of song as the sea, and our tongues of exultation as the multitude of its waves, and our lips of praise as the wide-extended firmament; though our eyes shone with light like the sun and the moon, and our hands were spread forth like the eagles of heaven, and our feet were swift as hinds, we should still be unable to thank thee and bless thy name, O Lord our God and God of our fathers, for one thousandth or one ten thousandth part of the bounties which thou has bestowed upon our fathers and upon us.

- from the Hebrew Prayer Book **Psalm 100**

Make a joyful noise to the Lord, all the lands! Serve the Lord with gladness! Come into God's presence with singing! Know that the Lord is God! It is he that made us, and we are his; we are his people, and the sheep of his pasture. Enter his gates with thanksgiving, and his courts with praise! Give thanks to him, bless his name! For the Lord is good; his steadfast love endures for ever, and his faithfulness to all generations.

Psalm 111

Praise the Lord. I will give thanks to the Lord with my whole heart, in the company of the upright, in the congregation. Great are the works of the Lord, studied by all who have pleasure in them. Full of honor and majesty is his work, and his righteousness endures for ever. He has caused his wonderful works to be remembered; the Lord is gracious and merciful. He provides food for those who fear him; he is ever mindful of his covenant. He has shown his people the power of his works, in giving them the heritage of the nations. The works of his hands are faithful and just; all his precepts are trustworthy, they are established for ever and ever, to be performed with faithfulness and uprightness. He sent redemption to his people; he has commanded his covenant for ever. Holy and terrible is his name! The fear of the Lord is the beginning of wisdom; a good understanding have all those who practice it. His praise endures for ever!

Moravian Blessing

Come, Lord Jesus, our guest to be And bless these gifts Bestowed by Thee. And bless our loved ones everywhere, And keep them in Your loving care.

Thanksgiving

For each new morning with its light, For rest and shelter of the night, For health and food, For love and friends, For everything Thy goodness sends.

- Ralph Waldo Emerson (1803-1882)

We Give Thanks

Our Father in Heaven, We give thanks for the pleasure Of gathering together for this occasion. We give thanks for this food Prepared by loving hands. We give thanks for life, The freedom to enjoy it all And all other blessings. As we partake of this food, We pray for health and strength To carry on and try to live as You would have us. This we ask in the name of Christ, Our Heavenly Father.

- Harry Jewell

O God of all Creation: You have cared for the earth, and have filled it with your riches. Abundance flows in your steppes, through the pastures and wilderness. You provide for our land, softening it with showers, bathing it in light, and blessing it with growth.

The hills sing with joy; the meadows are covered with flocks; the fields deck themselves with wheat; and together they glorify your name!

On this occasion of our Thanksgiving, we as a nation take rest from our labors to consider your many blessings. We thank you for our freedoms, and for the opportunity to contribute our skills, our attributes and our values toward the good of society.

We thank you for the mixture of our cultures, blending us into one people under God. Help us to be a light unto other nations, and to further the cause of freedom and justice all over the world.

We remember those who are less fortunate than we. We lift up in prayer the victims of poverty and racism, and all those who suffer from forms of political and economic oppression. Let the word that goes forth from our mouths speak of your peace, and let us proclaim our hope in Christ as Savior of all humankind.

We pray that you will bless all those who gather here, as we have come to experience your presence among us. Give us your guidance, O God, and empower us for your work. For we claim nothing for ourselves, but return all honor and glory unto you, and offer our thanks and praise. Amen.

From "Prayers for God's People "Thomas P. Roberts, editor

The Canticle of the Creatures

Most High, all-powerful, all-good Lord, All praise is Yours, all glory, honor and blessings. To you alone, Most High, do they belong; no mortal lips are worthy to pronounce Your Name. We praise You, Lord, for all Your creatures, especially for Brother Sun, who is the day through whom You give us light. And he is beautiful and radiant with great splendor, of You Most High, he bears your likeness. We praise You, Lord, for Sister Moon and the stars, in the heavens you have made them bright, precious and fair. We praise You, Lord, for Brothers Wind and Air, fair and stormy, all weather's moods, by which You cherish all that You have made. We praise You, Lord, for Sister Water, so useful, humble, precious and pure. We praise You, Lord, for Brother Fire, through whom You light the night. He is beautiful, playful, robust, and strong. We praise You, Lord, for Sister Earth, who sustains us with her fruits, colored flowers, and herbs. We praise You, Lord, for those who pardon, for love of You bear sickness and trial. Blessed are those who endure in peace, by You Most High, they will be crowned. We praise You, Lord, for Sister Death, from whom no-one living can escape. Woe to those who die in their sins! Blessed are those that She finds doing Your Will. No second death can do them harm. We praise and bless You, Lord, and give You thanks, and serve You in all humility.

-St. Francis of Assisi

Romans 8:17-23

17Now if we are children, then we are heirs—heirs of God and co-heirs with Christ, if indeed we share in his sufferings in order that we may also share in his glory.

Future Glory

18I consider that our present sufferings are not worth comparing with the glory that will be revealed in us. **19**The creation waits in eager expectation for the sons of God to be revealed. **20**For the creation was subjected to frustration, not by its own choice, but by the will of the one who subjected it, in hope **21**that[a] the creation itself will be liberated from its bondage to decay and brought into the glorious freedom of the children of God.**22**We know that the whole creation has been groaning as in the pains of childbirth right up to the present time. **23**Not only so, but we ourselves, who have the first fruits of the Spirit, groan inwardly as we wait eagerly for our adoption as sons, the redemption of our bodies.

Romans 8:26

In the same way, the Spirit helps us in our weakness. We do not know what we ought to pray for, but the Spirit himself intercedes for us with groans that words cannot express.

Although the Scriptures can provide inspiration for prayers, it is not important that we turn to God using flowery poetry and eloquent words. In our deepest despair, if we simply turn our hearts to God, we are engaged in prayer. And even if we continue to cry in the presence of God, we may be comforted that we are not, and never are, alone.

Intercessory Prayer

Intercessory prayers are prayers on behalf of others. We ask not for ourselves, but for them. We are all familiar with prayers of intercession and we offer them up frequently. Prayers may be offered in which you ask God for specific intercession, or your prayers may be more general such as: "God, be with ... this week" or "God, I commend to you ..." or "God, may ... know your hope."

A non-verbal way to pray for others is to use your imagination. In your mind's eye, visualize the person for whom you are praying, and then visualize him or her cured from whatever is afflicting him, or surrounded with the light of God's love, or in the company of Jesus. Allow the mental picture to take its own shape, and wish for God's blessing.

There are plenty of examples of intercession:

Genesis

New International Version (NIV)

23 Then Abraham approached him and said: "Will you sweep away the righteous with the wicked? **24** What if there are fifty righteous people in the city? Will you really sweep it away and not spare [a] the place for the sake of the fifty righteous people in it? **25** Far be it from you to do such a thing—to kill the righteous with the wicked, treating the righteous and the wicked alike. Far be it from you! Will not the Judge [b] of all the earth do right?"

26 The LORD said, "If I find fifty righteous people in the city of Sodom, I will spare the whole place for their sake."

27 Then Abraham spoke up again: "Now that I have been so bold as to speak to the Lord, though I am nothing but dust and ashes, **28** what if the number of the righteous is five less than fifty? Will you destroy the whole city because of five people?" "If I find forty-five there," he said, "I will not destroy it."

29 Once again he spoke to him, "What if only forty are found there?" He said, "For the sake of forty, I will not do it."

30 Then he said, "May the Lord not be angry, but let me speak. What if only thirty can be found there?" He answered, "I will not do it if I find thirty there."

31 Abraham said, "Now that I have been so bold as to speak to the Lord, what if only twenty can be found there?" He said, "For the sake of twenty, I will not destroy it."

32 Then he said, "May the Lord not be angry, but let me speak just once more. What if only ten can be found there?" He answered, "For the sake of ten, I will not destroy it."

Genesis 20:17
New International Version (NIV)

17 Then Abraham prayed to God, and God healed Abimelech, his wife and his slave girls so they could have children again

Genesis 49 (New International Version)

New International Version (NIV)

Genesis 49

Jacob Blesses His Sons

1 Then Jacob called for his sons and said: "Gather around so I can tell you what will happen to you in days to come.
2 "Assemble and listen, sons of Jacob; listen to your father Israel.
3 "Reuben, you are my firstborn, my might, the first sign of my strength, excelling in honor, excelling in power.
4 Turbulent as the waters, you will no longer excel, for you went up onto your father's bed, onto my couch and defiled

it.

5 "Simeon and Levi are brothers— their swords [a] are weapons of violence.

6 Let me not enter their council, let me not join their assembly, for they have killed men in their anger and hamstrung oxen as they pleased.

7 Cursed be their anger, so fierce, and their fury, so cruel! I will scatter them in Jacob and disperse them in Israel.

8 "Judah, [b] your brothers will praise you; your hand will be on the neck of your enemies; your father's sons will bow down to you.

9 You are a lion's cub, O Judah; you return from the prey, my son. Like a lion he crouches and lies down, like a lioness—who dares to rouse him?

10 The scepter will not depart from Judah, nor the ruler's staff from between his feet, until he comes to whom it belongs [c] and the obedience of the nations is his.

11 He will tether his donkey to a vine, his colt to the choicest branch; he will wash his garments in wine, his robes in the blood of grapes.

12 His eyes will be darker than wine, his teeth whiter than milk. [d]

13 "Zebulun will live by the seashore and become a haven for ships; his border will extend toward Sidon.

14 "Issachar is a rawboned [e] donkey lying down between two saddlebags. [f]

15 When he sees how good is his resting place and how pleasant is his land, he will bend his shoulder to the burden and submit to forced labor.

16 "Dan [g] will provide justice for his people as one of the tribes of Israel.

17 Dan will be a serpent by the roadside, a viper along the path, that bites the horse's heels so that its rider tumbles backward.

18 "I look for your deliverance, O LORD.

19 "Gad [h] will be attacked by a band of raiders, but he will attack them at their heels.

20 "Asher's food will be rich; he will provide delicacies fit for a king.

21 "Naphtali is a doe set free that bears beautiful fawns. [i]

22 "Joseph is a fruitful vine, a fruitful vine near a spring, whose branches climb over a wall. [j]

23 With bitterness archers attacked him; they shot at him with hostility.

24 But his bow remained steady, his strong arms stayed [k] limber, because of the hand of the Mighty One of Jacob, because of the Shepherd, the Rock of Israel,

25 because of your father's God, who helps you, because of the Almighty, [l] who blesses you with blessings of the heavens above, blessings of the deep that lies below, blessings of the breast and womb.

26 Your father's blessings are greater than the blessings of
the ancient mountains, than [m] the bounty of the age-old
hills. Let all these rest on the head of Joseph, on the brow
of the prince among [n] his brothers.
27 "Benjamin is a ravenous wolf; in the morning he
devours the prey, in the evening he divides the plunder."
28 All these are the twelve tribes of Israel, and this is what
their father said to them when he blessed them, giving each
the blessing appropriate to him.

The Death of Jacob

29 Then he gave them these instructions: "I am about to be
gathered to my people. Bury me with my fathers in the cave
in the field of Ephron the Hittite, **30** the cave in the field of
Machpelah, near Mamre in Canaan, which Abraham
bought as a burial place from Ephron the Hittite, along
with the field. **31** There Abraham and his wife Sarah were
buried, there Isaac and his wife Rebekah were buried, and
there I buried Leah. **32** The field and the cave in it were
bought from the Hittites. [o] "
33 When Jacob had finished giving instructions to his
sons, he drew his feet up into the bed, breathed his last and
was gathered to his people.

1 Kings 8:29-53 (New International Version)

New International Version (NIV)

29 May your eyes be open toward this temple night and day, this place of which you said, 'My Name shall be there,' so that you will hear the prayer your servant prays toward this place. **30** Hear the supplication of your servant and of your people Israel when they pray toward this place. Hear from heaven, your dwelling place, and when you hear, forgive.

31 "When a man wrongs his neighbor and is required to take an oath and he comes and swears the oath before your altar in this temple, **32** then hear from heaven and act. Judge between your servants, condemning the guilty and bringing down on his own head what he has done. Declare the innocent not guilty, and so establish his innocence.

33 "When your people Israel have been defeated by an enemy because they have sinned against you, and when they turn back to you and confess your name, praying and making supplication to you in this temple, **34** then hear from heaven and forgive the sin of your people Israel and bring them back to the land you gave to their fathers.

35 "When the heavens are shut up and there is no rain because your people have sinned against you, and when they pray toward this place and confess your name and turn from their sin because you have afflicted them, **36** then hear from heaven and forgive the sin of your servants, your people Israel. Teach them the right way to live, and send rain on the land you gave your people for an inheritance.

37 "When famine or plague comes to the land, or blight or mildew, locusts or grasshoppers, or when an enemy besieges them in any of their cities, whatever disaster or disease may come, **38** and when a prayer or plea is made by any of your people Israel—each one aware of the afflictions of his own heart, and spreading out his hands toward this temple- **39** then hear from heaven, your dwelling place. Forgive and act; deal with each man according to all he does, since you know his heart (for you alone know the hearts of all men), **40** so that they will fear you all the time they live in the land you gave our fathers.

41 "As for the foreigner who does not belong to your people Israel but has come from a distant land because of your name- **42** for men will hear of your great name and your mighty hand and your outstretched arm—when he comes and prays toward this temple, **43** then hear from heaven, your dwelling place, and do whatever the foreigner asks of you, so that all the peoples of the earth may know your name and fear you, as do your own people Israel, and may know that this house I have built bears your Name.

44 "When your people go to war against their enemies, wherever you send them, and when they pray to the LORD toward the city you have chosen and the temple I have built for your Name, **45** then hear from heaven their prayer and their plea, and uphold their cause.

46 "When they sin against you—for there is no one who does not sin—and you become angry with them and give them over to the enemy, who takes them captive to his own land, far away or near; **47** and if they have a change of heart in the land where they are held captive, and repent and plead with you in the land of their conquerors and say, 'We have sinned, we have done wrong, we have acted wickedly'; **48** and if they turn back to you with all their heart and soul in the land of their enemies who took them captive, and pray to you toward the land you gave their fathers, toward the city you have chosen and the temple I have built for your Name; **49** then from heaven, your dwelling place, hear their prayer and their plea, and uphold their cause. **50** And forgive your people, who have sinned against you; forgive all the offenses they have committed against you, and cause their conquerors to show them mercy; **51** for they are your people and your inheritance, whom you brought out of Egypt, out of that iron-smelting furnace.

52 "May your eyes be open to your servant's plea and to the plea of your people Israel, and may you listen to them whenever they cry out to you.

53 For you singled them out from all the nations of the world to be your own inheritance, just as you declared through your servant Moses when you, O Sovereign LORD, brought our fathers out of Egypt."

Matthew 17:15

"Lord, have mercy on my son," he said. "He has seizures and is suffering greatly. He often falls into the fire or into the water.

Mark 9:17-27

17A man in the crowd answered, "Teacher, I brought you my son, who is possessed by a spirit that has robbed him of speech.

18Whenever it seizes him, it throws him to the ground. He foams at the mouth, gnashes his teeth and becomes rigid. I asked your disciples to drive out the spirit, but they could not."

19"O unbelieving generation," Jesus replied, "how long shall I stay with you? How long shall I put up with you? Bring the boy to me."

20So they brought him. When the spirit saw Jesus, it immediately threw the boy into a convulsion. He fell to the ground and rolled around, foaming at the mouth.

21Jesus asked the boy's father, "How long has he been like this?" "From childhood," he answered.

22"It has often thrown him into fire or water to kill him. But if you can do anything, take pity on us and help us."

23" 'If you can'?" said Jesus. "Everything is possible for him who believes."

24Immediately the boy's father exclaimed, "I do believe; help me overcome my unbelief!"

25When Jesus saw that a crowd was running to the scene, he rebuked the evil[a] spirit. "You deaf and mute spirit," he said, "I command you, come out of him and never enter him again."

26The spirit shrieked, convulsed him violently and came out. The boy looked so much like a corpse that many said, "He's dead."

27But Jesus took him by the hand and lifted him to his feet, and he stood up.

Matthew 15:22 (New International Version)

22A Canaanite woman from that vicinity came to him, crying out, "Lord, Son of David, have mercy on me! My daughter is suffering terribly from demon-possession."

Genesis 18:23-32 Then Abraham approached him and said: "Will you sweep away the righteous with the wicked? What if there are fifty righteous people in the city? Will you really sweep it away and not spare the place for the sake of the fifty righteous people in it? Far be it from you to do such a thing—to kill the righteous with the wicked, treating the righteous and the wicked alike. Far be it from you! Will not the Judge of all the earth do right?" The LORD said, "If I find fifty righteous people in the city of Sodom, I will spare the whole place for their sake." Then Abraham spoke up again: "Now that I have been so bold as to speak to the Lord, though I am nothing but dust and ashes, what if the number of the righteous is five less than fifty? Will you destroy the whole city because of five people?" "If I find forty-five there," he said, "I will not destroy it." Once again he spoke to him, "What if only forty are found there?" He said, "For the sake of forty, I will not do it." Then he said, "May the Lord not be angry, but let me speak. What if only thirty can be found there?" He answered, "I will not do it if

111

I find thirty there." Abraham said, "Now that I have been so bold as to speak to the Lord, what if only twenty can be found there?" He said, "For the sake of twenty, I will not destroy it." Then he said, "May the Lord not be angry, but let me speak just once more. What if only ten can be found there?" He answered, "For the sake of ten, I will not destroy it."

2 Chronicles 7:14-15 If my people, who are called by my name, will humble themselves and pray and seek my face and turn from their wicked ways, then will I hear from heaven and will forgive their sin and will heal their land. Now my eyes will be open and my ears attentive to the prayers offered in this places are upon you."

Ezra 10:1 While Ezra was praying and confessing, weeping and throwing himself down before the house of God, a large crowd of Israelites—men, women and children—gathered around him. They too wept bitterly.

Nehemiah 9:32 "Now therefore, O our God, the great, mighty and awesome God, who keeps his covenant of love, do not let all this hardship seem trifling in your eyes--the hardship that has come upon us, upon our kings and leaders, upon our priests and prophets, upon our fathers and all your people, from the days of the kings of Assyria until today.

Psalms 106:23 So he said he would destroy them— had not Moses, his chosen one, stood in the breach before him to keep his wrath from destroying them.

Isaiah 59:16 He saw that there was no one, he was appalled that there was no one to intervene; so his own arm worked salvation for him, and his own righteousness sustained him.

Isaiah 62:6-7 I have posted watchmen on your walls, O Jerusalem; they will never be silent day or night. You who call on the LORD, give yourselves no rest and give him no rest till he establishes Jerusalem and makes her the praise of the earth.

Ezekiel 22:30-31 I looked for a man among them who would build up the wall and stand before me in the gap on behalf of the land so I would not have to destroy it, but I found none. So I will pour out my wrath on them and consume them with my fiery anger, bringing down on their own heads all they have done, declares the Sovereign LORD.

Daniel 6:10 Now when Daniel learned that the decree had been published, he went home to his upstairs room where the windows opened toward Jerusalem. Three times a day he got down on his knees and prayed, giving thanks to his God, just as he had done before.

Jeremiah 13:16-17 Give glory to the LORD your God before he brings the darkness, before your feet stumble on the darkening hills. You hope for light, but he will turn it to thick darkness and change it to deep gloom. But if you do not listen, I will weep in secret because of your pride; my eyes will weep bitterly, overflowing with tears, because the LORD's flock will be taken captive.

Lamentations 3:48-50 Streams of tears flow from my eyes because my people are destroyed. My eyes will flow unceasingly, without relief, until the LORD looks down from heaven and sees.

Joel 2:17 Let the priests, who minister before the LORD, weep between the temple porch and the altar. Let them say, "Spare your people, O LORD. Do not make your inheritance an object of scorn, a byword among the nations. Why should they say among the peoples, 'Where is their God?'

Luke 22:32 But I have prayed for you, Simon, that your faith may not fail. And when you have turned back, strengthen your brothers."

John 17:1-26 After Jesus said this, he looked toward heaven and prayed: "Father, the time has come. Glorify your Son, that your Son may glorify you. For you granted him authority over all people that he might give eternal life to all those you have given him. Now this is eternal life: that they may know you, the only true God, and Jesus Christ, whom you have sent. I have brought you glory on earth by completing the work you gave me to do. And now, Father, glorify me in your presence with the glory I had with you before the world began. "I have revealed you to those whom you gave me out of the world. They were yours; you gave them to me and they have obeyed your word. Now they know that everything you have given me comes from you. For I gave them the words you gave me and they accepted them. They knew with certainty that I came from you, and they believed that you sent me. I pray for them. I am not praying for the world, but for those you have given me, for they are yours. All I have is yours, and all you have is mine. And glory has come to me through them. I will remain in the world no longer, but they are still in the world, and I am coming to you. Holy Father, protect them by the power of your name--the name you gave me-- so that they may be one as we are one. While I was with them, I protected them and kept them safe by that name you gave me. None has been lost except the one doomed to destruction so that Scripture would be fulfilled. "I am coming to you now, but I say these things while I am still in the world, so that they may have the full measure of my joy within them. I have given them your word and the world has hated them, for they are not of the world any more than I am of the world. My prayer is not that you take them out of the world but that you protect them from the evil one. They are not of the world, even as I am not of it. Sanctify them by the truth; your word is truth. As you sent me into the world, I have sent them into the world. For them I sanctify myself, that they too may be truly sanctified. "My prayer is not for them alone. I pray also for those who will believe in me through their message, that all of them may be one, Father, just as you are in me and I am in you. May they also be in us so that the world may believe that you have sent me. I have given them the glory that you gave me, that they may be one as we are one: I in them and you in me. May they be brought to complete unity to let the world know that you sent me and have loved them even as you have loved me. "Father, I want those you have given me to be with me where I am, and to see my glory, the glory you have given me because you loved me before the creation of the world. "Righteous Father, though the world does not know you, I know you, and they know that you have sent me. I have made you known to them, and will continue to make you known in order that the love you have for me may be in them and that I myself may be in them."

Acts 12:5-12 So Peter was kept in prison, but the church was earnestly praying to God for him. The night before Herod was to bring him to trial, Peter was sleeping between two soldiers, bound with two chains, and sentries stood guard at the entrance. Suddenly an angel of the Lord appeared and a light shone in the cell. He struck Peter on the side and woke him up. "Quick, get up!" he said, and the chains fell off Peter's wrists. Then the angel said to him, "Put on your clothes and sandals." And Peter did so. "Wrap your cloak around you and follow me," the angel told him. Peter followed him out of the prison, but he had no idea that what the angel was doing was really happening; he thought he was seeing a vision. They passed the first and second guards and came to the iron gate leading to the city. It opened for them by itself, and they went through it. When they had walked the length of one street, suddenly the angel left him. Then Peter came to himself and said, "Now I know without a doubt that the Lord sent his angel and rescued me from Herod's clutches and from everything the Jewish people were anticipating." When this had dawned on him, he went to the house of Mary the mother of John, also called Mark, where many people had gathered and were praying.

Romans 8:26 In the same way, the Spirit helps us in our weakness. We do not know what we ought to pray for, but the Spirit himself intercedes for us with groans that words cannot express

1 Timothy 2:1-4 I urge, then, first of all, that requests, prayers, intercession and thanksgiving be made for everyone— for kings and all those in authority, that we may live peaceful and quiet lives in all godliness and holiness. This is good, and pleases God our Savior, who wants all men to be saved and to come to a knowledge of the truth.

Hebrews 5:7 During the days of Jesus' life on earth, he offered up prayers and petitions with loud cries and tears to the one who could save him from death, and he was heard because of his reverent submission.

Hebrews 7:23-25 Now there have been many of those priests, since death prevented them from continuing in office; but because Jesus lives forever, he has a permanent priesthood. Therefore he is able to save completel those who come to God through him, because he always lives to intercede for them.

James 5:13-16 Is any one of you in trouble? He should pray. Is anyone happy? Let him sing songs of praise. Is any one of you sick? He should call the elders of the church to pray over him and anoint him with oil in the name of the Lord. And the prayer offered in faith will make the sick person well; the Lord will raise him up. If he has sinned, he will be forgiven. Therefore confess your sins to each other and pray for each other so that you may be healed. The prayer of a righteous man is powerful and effective.

Appropriateness of Prayers of Intercession

Prayers of intercession, you will notice, have some common thematic elements.

They do not beseech God for vengeance, material wealth, or anything counter to His teachings. Prayers of intercession are selfless, and are not grounded in desires for earthly possessions or wealth.

Prayer is certainly appropriate. But as New Testament Believers, Christians are called upon to be a "living sacrifice" to God. Prayer is only part of the manner in which a Christian can devote him or herself to God. Doing good works on His behalf to help others is an excellent supplement to prayer. Donating to charity, volunteering your time at a non-profit organization, offering childcare to a struggling family, or otherwise being helpful to the needy are ways in which God can see your devotion to your request for His intercession.

PRAYER OF CENTERING

Most forms of prayer teach us ways to speak to God, not ways to listen to God. To listen effectively we must be willing to be silent. Centering prayer is a form of prayer that helps us be still and listen to God.

Seeds of the ideas behind contemplation can be found early in the Christian era. The first appearance contemplative prayer appears in the 4th century writings of the monk St. John Cassian, who wrote of a practice he learned from Isaac. It can thus be argued that contemplation was among the earliest meditational and/or devotional practice of Christian monasticism, being later supplanted in dominance by the scholastic theologians.

The Trappist monk and influential theologian Thomas Merton was strongly influenced by Buddhist meditation, and his writing and teaching attempted to unify existentialism with philosophies of the Roman Catholic faith. He was also a believer of meditation and contemplative prayer.

The practice of centering prayer is the commitment to simply be with God in silence for 15 or 20 minutes once or twice a day. This practice is much like meditation. In order to begin, it is recommended that you select a sacred word or phrase, from Scripture if you wish, to chant to yourself.

Once you have chosen your word or image and have repeated it enough times to feel ready to listen, begin your prayer time with a brief prayer asking God's guidance and then simply sit silently in God's presence. Do your best to silence the inner chatter of your brain by immediately going back to your sacred word or phrase whenever you are distracted.

Sometimes people think that the goal of centering prayer is to silence all thoughts and be in perfect stillness. The only of centering prayer is to be with God. After 15 or 20 minutes have passed, offer a brief prayer of thanksgiving, or say the Lord's Prayer, and move gently back into the activities of your life.

There are a variety of yoga studios, tai chi studios, and schools that offer courses in meditation, which may be a good idea for those having trouble with contemplative prayer. Misconceptions of meditation and other Eastern practices abound, so many Christians may be reluctant to engage in an activity associated with other faiths.

"Meditation" merely describes a state of purposeful, often

self-induced, state of concentration. Sometimes the purpose of meditation involves the pursuit of completely clearing the mind; other times it focuses on a specific object of thought or awareness. In this case, the goal is to seek solace in a direct connection with God, or to be aware of His presence. It usually involves turning the attention inward to a single point of reference. Meditation has been practiced in the East for thousands of years. The word "meditation" in the West has come to describe a wide variety of spiritual activities that emphasize stillness, concentration, or heightened self awareness.

Though meditation can be practiced alone, some prefer to engage in a practice referred to as "guided" meditation. In this practice, a priestess, priest, guru, teacher, spiritual authority, or spiritual leader guides the subject into a state of self-awareness and deep relaxation. The meditation leader may begin by asking the subject, or subjects, to bring awareness to the physical body to scan for any tension. The subjects will usually be asked to do this with their eyes closed. Next, the leader will lead the subjects through a series of visualizations. The intention is to get the subjects to focus on the task at hand, and strive for stillness and self-awareness.

Some consider a yoga class, for example, to be a form of guided meditation, in which the teacher takes the class through a series of movements to bring peace, comfort, and alignment to the physical body. Doing so will free the spiritual body and mind of earthly distractions, and liberate the subject for deep relaxation.

Meditation can also be guided with the help of a CD or audio recording. Guided meditation is not just for beginners. There are experienced practitioners of meditation who prefer to be guided so as to liberate themselves from the work of maintaining focus, or thinking of a path of visualization. There are meditation classes offered at community colleges, yoga centers, or even on line or via packages of CDs. It is not necessary to start meditating in a guided setting, but may be useful for the beginner so he or she will know what the goal is, and what sorts of challenges to expect.

Ultimately, the goal of meditation is to free the mind from clutter and achieve absolute stillness of the mind. This will allow the self to become open to experiencing the collective unconscious, and exist in a state of pure and total awareness.

Lectio Divina

Another prayer form, Lectio Divina (which means Sacred Reading), uses Scripture to guide us into prayer. The principles of Lectio Divina were expressed around the year 220 AD by Origen. He wrote that in order to gain God's wisdom when reading from the Bible, it is necessary to do so with attention, constancy, focus, and prayer. Origen also emphasized the value of reading scripture with attention to possible different levels of meaning.

The systematization of spiritual reading into four steps dates back to the 12th century. Around 1150, Guigo II, a Carthusian monk, wrote a book titled "The Monk's Ladder" (Scala Claustralium) wherein he set out the theory of the four rungs: reading, meditation, prayer and contemplation.

In Lectio Divina the Scripture passage is read four times, with purpose and intention.. The first reading is read aloud to simply hear the words. The second reading, either aloud or silent, is for meditating on and really thinking about the passage. Try to think of the way in which the Words can be applied to your own life. If you have questions as to its meaning in general, or its meaning for you, think of these questions for as long as you wish. After the third reading, pray to God. Talk to God about what you have read and how you feel about it. When you read the passage the fourth time, allow the words to touch your heart. Then sit quietly and absorb the Word.

Praying in Groups

Prayer partners are one way to make a human commitment as well as a commitment to God. Praying can be alone, with a couple, or in large groups. Prayer partners can also be committed to praying for each other for a period of time. Sometimes prayer partnerships can serve the purpose of spiritual support, and be a foundation for discussion about God, His Words, and His will.

There are plenty of examples of group prayer in the Bible:

Zechariah 13:9
I will bring that group through the fire and make them pure, just as gold and silver are refined and purified by fire. They will call on my name, and I will answer them. I will say, 'These are my people,' and they will say, 'The LORD is our God.'

I Kings 18:36-39 And it came to pass, at the time of the offering of the evening sacrifice, that Elijah the prophet came near and said, "LORD God of Abraham, Isaac, and Israel, let it be known this day that You are God in Israel and I am Your servant, and that I have done all these things at Your word. Hear me, O LORD, hear me, that this people may know that You are the LORD God, and that You have turned their hearts back to You again."

Then the fire of the LORD fell and consumed the burnt sacrifice, and the wood and the stones and the dust, and it licked up the water that was in the trench. Now when all the people saw it, they fell on their faces; and they said, "The LORD, He is God! The LORD, He is God!" (NKJV)

2 Chronicles 20:18 (New International Version)

18 Jehoshaphat bowed with his face to the ground, and all the people of Judah and Jerusalem fell down in worship before the LORD.

If you choose to host a prayer group, or meet informally with others outside of a Church setting, you may be at a loss as to how to structure the prayer time.

Most prayer group activities are done in a ring or circle. This way, ach one faces most of the others, and can make eye contact if desired. It fosters a feeling of connection and oneness with others in the group, a feeling that becomes even more so when the hands are linked. The procedure that most people find most natural is to stand together in a ring, and have each person share, then going to the next person in the ring, until done. If hands are linked, one person can pass their turn on to the next simply by squeezing the next person's hand or softly saying something. Another common way is for each to share freely, in no particular order, waiting until the person speaking is done. Those who have experience in leading groups say that these are fine ways to begin, but it tends to become a rut, or attention spans are challenged, particularly if you are trying to conduct a prayer group that includes families and children.

Thus, other methods of sharing may be preferable, particularly if the group is large or the schedule doesn't allow for each person to freely share without worrying about the passage of time.

Sentence prayers: each person, one at a time, offers a brief specific concern, praise, or thanks to God, ending with "Amen" or some other refrain. No explaining it, just saying it and leaving it. (Allow those who don't want to share to say just "Amen" so it passes on to the next person.)

Silent intercessions: The leader reads a general concern, and is then silent. Time is then taken to silently pray for specific people, actions, and ministries involved with that general concern. Then, after a while, the leader speaks a word of the Bible relating to that concern, and a brief prayer on it.

Basket of prayer: each person writes just one concern that is most on their heart, onto a slip of paper. The papers are gathered in a basket, and the group prays over them. This can be done by reading each one or leaving them unread all together in the basket.

Prayer for witness: Each person in the group names *one* person that they most want to see turn to Christ. This would be someone from work, hobbies, family, or other non-religious activities, that they meet in the course of their daily lives. After each one is spoken, the group then prays for an opportunity for a Christian's witness to hit home.

Two-by-two: at the start, names are randomly drawn to be matched in pairs. The pairs then go to separate locations from the other pairs (like, say, one in the kitchen, another on the deck, another in the garden, etc.). The pair then takes time to minister, share, and pray with each other.

Echos: Someone speaks a phrase of Psalm or hymn or a very specific prayer. Then each person repeats the phrase, with short breaks in between each time it is spoken. This gives everyone time to think on the phrase, or to silently let it sink in, listening for some stirrings within.

Groups confessing: one approach is for a leader to talk briefly about a general kind or category of sin. All those present write onto slips of paper a few words of a specific instance where they committed that kind of sin. These are *not* to be read by anyone; this is between them and God. The papers are then gathered into a cooking container. All those present gather around it, and speak together a prayer of confession of being sorry for that kind of sin and expressing the determination to cease that sin. Then all take the container to a <u>safe</u> place indoors or outdoors, and then someone lights it, allowing it to burn completely to ash. (Have something to douse or smother it with in case of flare-up.) Once this is done, someone then says that these sins are forgiven due to Christ's work on the cross.

Strong personal needs: Sometimes, in a group setting, someone will be so hurt by life (or so moved by the group or its actions) that they will break down. Other times, composure will hold, but the need for prayer is acute and prayer is requested. Either way, see to it that the person is sitting down securely. (This sitting is known in some circles as the 'hot seat'.) Ask that person to start praying. Then bring the others present to gather around him/her, laying hands and praying until a sense of comfort about the matter comes over him/her, or that person brings it to an end.

Written prayers: Those in liturgical churches know these from worship services. A petition is offered, then ended with a clear ending tag, like, "O Lord" or "in Jesus' name", followed by a standard response spoken by all, such as "hear our prayer" or "let it happen, Lord". Then the next written petition is spoken, and so on. (The tags and response can be much less mundane than that. But simple often works best.)

This can be prevented by creating a structure in which a broad range of concerns are addressed each meeting. Most common is to start with praise, then introspective and contemplative prayer, then move to prayers for self and family, then intercessions for each other and the faith challenges/opportunities faced each day, then the congregation, then the community at large, the nation, and the world. Then, bring the focus back down to one: Jesus. Then, end with prayers of thanks and praise.

INCORPORATING PRAYER INTO YOUR LIFE

Even though we may feel strong conviction in the power of prayer, it still may be difficult to develop the discipline for constant prayer. In these times, trust in God is of the utmost importance.

There are times when God seems very far away and we feel very alone. We pray, we do our best to carry out his will and his works, but we still don't really know what he wants for us or what our true path is. In times like these, prayer is the key to sustaining your faith. Trust that God will show you His will and His way. Again, the Bible has much to say about trust in God:

"Trust in the Lord with all thine heart; and lean not unto thine own understanding." (Proverbs 3:5)

As for God, his way is perfect; the word of the Lord is tried: he is a buckler to all that trust in him." (II Samuel 22:31)

And this is the record, that God hath given to us eternal life, and this life is in his Son. He that hath the Son hath life; and he that hath not the Son of God hath not life." (I John 5:11-12)

135

And when they prevailed over them, the Hagrites and all who were with them were given into their hands, for they cried out to God in the battle, and he granted their urgent plea because they trusted in him.

—*1 Chronicles 5:20*

And those who know your name put their trust in you, for you, O Lord, have not forsaken those who seek you.

—*Psalm 9:10*

Many are the sorrows of the wicked, but steadfast love surrounds the one who trusts in the Lord.

—*Psalm 32:10*

Trust in the Lord, and do good; dwell in the land and befriend faithfulness. Delight yourself in the Lord, and he will give you the desires of your heart.

Commit your way to the Lord; trust in him, and he will act. He will bring forth your righteousness as the light, and your justice as the noonday.

—*Psalm 37:3-6*

He who dwells in the shelter of the Most High will abide in the shadow of the Almighty. I will say to the Lord, "My refuge and my fortress, my God, in whom I trust." For he will deliver you from the snare of the fowler and from the deadly pestilence. He will cover you with his pinions, and under his wings you will find refuge; his faithfulness is a shield and buckler. You will not fear the terror of the night, nor the arrow that flies by day, nor the pestilence that stalks in darkness, nor the destruction that wastes at noonday.

A thousand may fall at your side, ten thousand at your right hand, but it will not come near you. You will only look with your eyes and see the recompense of the wicked. Because you have made the Lord your dwelling place— the Most High, who is my refuge— no evil shall be allowed to befall you, no plague come near your tent.

For he will command his angels concerning you to guard you in all your ways. On their hands they will bear you up, lest you strike your foot against a stone. You will tread on the lion and the adder; the young lion and the serpent you will trample underfoot.

"Because he holds fast to me in love, I will deliver him; I will protect him, because he knows my name. When he calls to me, I will answer him; I will be with him in trouble; I will rescue him and honor him. With long life I will satisfy him and show him my salvation."
—*Psalm 91*

The Lord is on my side; I will not fear. What can man do to me? The Lord is on my side as my helper; I shall look in triumph on those who hate me.

It is better to take refuge in the Lord than to trust in man. It is better to take refuge in the Lord than to trust in princes.
—*Psalm 118:6-9*

Those who trust in the Lord are like Mount Zion, which cannot be moved, but abides forever. As the mountains surround Jerusalem, so the Lord surrounds his people, from this time forth and forevermore.
—*Psalm 125:1-2*

Trust in the Lord with all your heart, and do not lean on your own understanding. In all your ways acknowledge him, and he will make straight your paths.
—*Proverbs 3:5-6*

The fear of man lays a snare, but whoever trusts in the
Lord is safe.
—*Proverbs 29:25*

You will say in that day: "I will give thanks to you, O Lord,
for though you were angry with me, your anger turned
away, that you might comfort me.

"Behold, God is my salvation; I will trust, and will not be
afraid; for the Lord God is my strength and my song, and
he has become my salvation."
—*Isaiah 12:1-2*

You keep him in perfect peace whose mind is stayed on
you, because he trusts in you. Trust in the Lord forever, for
the Lord God is an everlasting rock.
—*Isaiah 26:3-4*

Thus says the Lord: "Cursed is the man who trusts in man
and makes flesh his strength, whose heart turns away from
the Lord. He is like a shrub in the desert, and shall not see
any good come. He shall dwell in the parched places of the
wilderness, in an uninhabited salt land.

"Blessed is the man who trusts in the Lord, whose trust is
the Lord. He is like a tree planted by water, that sends out

its roots by the stream, and does not fear when heat comes, for its leaves remain green, and is not anxious in the year of drought, for it does not cease to bear fruit."
—*Jeremiah 17:5-8*

And after he had dismissed the crowds, he went up on the mountain by himself to pray. When evening came, he was there alone, but the boat by this time was a long way from the land, beaten by the waves, for the wind was against them. And in the fourth watch of the night he came to them, walking on the sea. But when the disciples saw him walking on the sea, they were terrified, and said, "It is a ghost!" and they cried out in fear. But immediately Jesus spoke to them, saying, "Take heart; it is I. Do not be afraid."

And Peter answered him, "Lord, if it is you, command me to come to you on the water." He said, "Come." So Peter got out of the boat and walked on the water and came to Jesus. But when he saw the wind, he was afraid, and beginning to sink he cried out, "Lord, save me." Jesus immediately reached out his hand and took hold of him, saying to him, "O you of little faith, why did you doubt?" And when they got into the boat, the wind ceased. And those in the boat worshiped him, saying, "Truly you are the Son of God."
—*Matthew 14:23-33*

At that time the disciples came to Jesus, saying, "Who is the greatest in the kingdom of heaven?" And calling to him a child, he put him in the midst of them and said, "Truly, I say to you, unless you turn and become like children, you will never enter the kingdom of heaven. Whoever humbles himself like this child is the greatest in the kingdom of heaven.

"Whoever receives one such child in my name receives me, but whoever causes one of these little ones who believe in me to sin, it would be better for him to have a great millstone fastened around his neck and to be drowned in the depth of the sea.
—*Matthew 18:1-6*

So also the chief priests, with the scribes and elders, mocked him, saying, "He saved others; he cannot save himself. He is the King of Israel; let him come down now from the cross, and we will believe in him. He trusts in God; let God deliver him now, if he desires him. For he said, 'I am the Son of God.'" And the robbers who were crucified with him also reviled him in the same way.
—*Matthew 27:41-44*

And when Jesus had crossed again in the boat to the other side, a great crowd gathered about him, and he was beside the sea. Then came one of the rulers of the synagogue, Jairus by name, and seeing him, he fell at his feet and implored him earnestly, saying, "My little daughter is at the point of death. Come and lay your hands on her, so that she may be made well and live." And he went with him. And a great crowd followed him and thronged about him. While he was still speaking, there came from the ruler's house some who said, "Your daughter is dead. Why trouble the Teacher any further?" But overhearing what they said, Jesus said to the ruler of the synagogue, "Do not fear, only believe." And he allowed no one to follow him except Peter and James and John the brother of James. They came to the house of the ruler of the synagogue, and Jesus saw a commotion, people weeping and wailing loudly. And when he had entered, he said to them, "Why are you making a commotion and weeping? The child is not dead but sleeping." And they laughed at him. But he put them all outside and took the child's father and mother and those who were with him and went in where the child was. Taking her by the hand he said to her, "Talitha cumi," which means, "Little girl, I say to you, arise." And immediately the girl got up and began walking (for she was twelve years of age), and they were immediately overcome with amazement. And he strictly charged them that no one should know this, and told them to give her something to eat.

—*Mark 5:21-24, 35-43*

And when Jesus had crossed again in the boat to the other side, a great crowd gathered about him, and he was beside the sea. Then came one of the rulers of the synagogue, Jairus by name, and seeing him, he fell at his feet and implored him earnestly, saying, "My little daughter is at the point of death. Come and lay your hands on her, so that she may be made well and live." And he went with him. And a great crowd followed him and thronged about him. While he was still speaking, there came from the ruler's house some who said, "Your daughter is dead. Why trouble the Teacher any further?" But overhearing what they said, Jesus said to the ruler of the synagogue, "Do not fear, only believe." And he allowed no one to follow him except Peter and James and John the brother of James. They came to the house of the ruler of the synagogue, and Jesus saw a commotion, people weeping and wailing loudly. And when he had entered, he said to them, "Why are you making a commotion and weeping? The child is not dead but sleeping." And they laughed at him. But he put them all outside and took the child's father and mother and those who were with him and went in where the child was. Taking her by the hand he said to her, "Talitha cumi," which means, "Little girl, I say to you, arise." And immediately the girl got up and began walking (for she was twelve years of age), and they were immediately overcome with amazement. And he strictly charged them that no one should know this, and told them to give her something to eat.

—*Mark 5:21-24, 35-43*

So he came again to Cana in Galilee, where he had made the water wine. And at Capernaum there was an official whose son was ill. When this man heard that Jesus had come from Judea to Galilee, he went to him and asked him to come down and heal his son, for he was at the point of death. So Jesus said to him, "Unless you see signs and wonders you will not believe." The official said to him, "Sir, come down before my child dies." Jesus said to him, "Go; your son will live." The man believed the word that Jesus spoke to him and went on his way. As he was going down, his servants met him and told him that his son was recovering. So he asked them the hour when he began to get better, and they said to him, "Yesterday at the seventh hour the fever left him." The father knew that was the hour when Jesus had said to him, "Your son will live." And he himself believed, and all his household.

—*John 4:46-53*

What if some were unfaithful? Does their faithlessness nullify the faithfulness of God? By no means! Let God be true though every one were a liar, as it is written, "That you may be justified in your words, and prevail when you are judged."

—*Romans 3:3-4*

For what does the Scripture say? "Abraham believed God, and it was counted to him as righteousness." Now to the one who works, his wages are not counted as a gift but as his due. And to the one who does not work but believes in him who justifies the ungodly, his faith is counted as righteousness,

—*Romans 4:3-5*

For what does the Scripture say? "Abraham believed God, and it was counted to him as righteousness." Now to the one who works, his wages are not counted as a gift but as his due. And to the one who does not work but believes in him who justifies the ungodly, his faith is counted as righteousness,

—*Romans 4:3-5*

For I am sure that neither death nor life, nor angels nor rulers, nor things present nor things to come, nor powers, nor height nor depth, nor anything else in all creation, will be able to separate us from the love of God in Christ Jesus our Lord.

—*Romans 8:38-39*

For I am sure that neither death nor life, nor angels nor rulers, nor things present nor things to come, nor powers, nor height nor depth, nor anything else in all creation, will be able to separate us from the love of God in Christ Jesus our Lord.

—*Romans 8:38-39*

May the God of hope fill you with all joy and peace in believing, so that by the power of the Holy Spirit you may abound in hope.

—*Romans 15:13*

May the God of hope fill you with all joy and peace in believing, so that by the power of the Holy Spirit you may abound in hope.

—*Romans 15:13*

Indeed, we felt that we had received the sentence of death. But that was to make us rely not on ourselves but on God who raises the dead.
—*2 Corinthians 1:9*

For the Son of God, Jesus Christ, whom we proclaimed among you, Silvanus and Timothy and I, was not Yes and No, but in him it is always Yes. For all the promises of God find their Yes in him. That is why it is through him that we utter our Amen to God for his glory.
—*2 Corinthians 1:19-20*

And I am sure of this, that he who began a good work in you will bring it to completion at the day of Jesus Christ.
—*Philippians 1:6*

which is why I suffer as I do. But I am not ashamed, for I know whom I have believed, and I am convinced that he is able to guard until that Day what has been entrusted to me.
—*2 Timothy 1:12*

And this is the confidence that we have toward him, that if we ask anything according to his will he hears us. And if we know that he hears us in whatever we ask, we know that we have the requests that we have asked of him.
—*1 John 5:14-15*

And this is the confidence that we have toward him, that if we ask anything according to his will he hears us. And if we know that he hears us in whatever we ask, we know that we have the requests that we have asked of him.

—*1 John 5:14-15*

And this is the confidence that we have toward him, that if we ask anything according to his will he hears us. And if we know that he hears us in whatever we ask, we know that we have the requests that we have asked of him.

—*1 John 5:14-15*

If you find that you are having a tough time devoting yourself to prayer, the Scripture, and God, there are ways to get yourself back on the path of God.

*talk to a church leader
*get involved with church activities
*if you are unhappy with your church, make an effort to find another
*make a prayer date with a prayer buddy
*take time to yourself to meditate on God
*talk to someone who has perhaps experienced a similar crisis of faith.

And remember, there are plenty of ways to pray. There are as many ways to pray as there are people.

-Incorporate your family into your prayer.
If you pray as a family, it will become part of everyone's routine. The discipline involved in setting aside time for prayer may be easier if it is just seen as part of the daily routine to pray together.

-Do activities mindfully, and they too can be prayer. Going to the gym, engaging in Christ-centered yoga, gardening, going for a walk—all of these activities can be prayer.

-constantly remember what you have to be thankful for. Remember, giving thanks is a form of prayer.

No matter what you go through, remember that God is with you. God bless.

SARAH PALIN, GOD & PRAYER

About her 5th Child:

http://lifenews.com/state3150.html

"We knew through early testing he would face special challenges, and we feel privileged that God would entrust us with this gift and allow us unspeakable joy as he entered our lives," she said.

'We have faith that every baby is created for good purpose and has potential to make this world a better place. We are truly blessed," the 44 year-old governor added.

From the Alaska Assemblies of God newsletter:

The opening night banquet of the 2008 Alaska District Council was honored to have Governor Sarah Palin address the delegates and guests. Governor Palin spoke of her appreciation for the Assemblies of God and requested that the Council pray for both her and the State of Alaska. Superintendent Ted Boatsman, who was Palin's junior high pastor at Wasilla Assembly of God, along with Pastor Mike Rose of Juneau Christian Center, where Palin presently attends church when in Juneau, laid hands on the Governor and led the Council in prayer.

Palin, who was elected Governor in 2007, is Alaska's youngest governor and the first female governor of the state. She just recently gave birth to her fifth child, Trig. Palin spoke of the faith challenge she faced when learning that Trig would be a Downs Syndrome child. However, she and her husband, Todd, believe that every child is a gift of God, deserving of life, and that God was asking them to accept His will for their lives. The Alaska District Council believes that the State of Alaska is blessed to have a woman of faith and courage as Governor.

Anchorage Daily News in 2006:

Palin's parents say they are not political and don't know how she decided to turn her ambition and work ethic toward politics. Her Christian faith, they say, came from her mother, who took her children to area Bible churches as they were growing up (Sarah is the third of four siblings). They say her faith has been steady since high school, when she led the Fellowship of Christian Athletes, and grew stronger as she sought out believers in her college years.

Palin doesn't brandish her religion on the campaign trail, but that doesn't prevent others from doing so. After she was first elected mayor, her predecessor, John Stein, objected that a Valley cable TV program had hailed her as Wasilla's first "Christian mayor." In a column for the local newspaper, he named eight previous mayors and added that he, too, was a Christian, despite a name that led some voters to suspect "I must be a non-Christian, have non-Christian blood or at least have sympathized with a non-Christian sometime in my career."

Time Magazine Interview August 14, 2008:

In an interview Palin did with Time magazine on August 14, 2008, Palin identified herself simply as a "Bible-believing Christian" who attends a "nondenominational Bible church." She says she was baptized in the Catholic church as an infant, but that her family began attending nondenominational churches thereafter. Here's the relevant snippet from the interview transcript:

[TIME:] Where do you see yourself going? Staying on in Alaska. Washington?

[Palin:] You know, I don't know. I knew early on that the smartest thing for me to do was to work hard, do the best that I can, make wise decisions based on good information in front of me. And then put my life, get myself on a path that could be dedicated to God and ask Him what I should next. That will be the position I will be in as long as I'm on earth — that is, seeking the right path that God would have laid out for me.

[TIME:] What's your religion?

[Palin:] Christian.

[TIME:] Any particular...?

[Palin:] No. Bible-believing Christian.

[TIME:] What church do you attend?

[Palin:] A non-denominational Bible church. I was baptized Catholic as a newborn and then my family started going to non-denominational churches throughout our life.

On abortion, same-sex marriage, and teaching "alternatives to evolution (such as creationism and intelligent design)" in public schools:

(Associated Baptist Press, August 29, 2008, and Anchorage Daily News , October 25, 2006)

While social issues are rarely election-deciders in libertarian-leaning Alaska, Palin has expressed strong opposition to gay rights. Besides supporting [a state constitutional amendment banning same-sex-marriage], she also said, during her 2006 campaign, that she disapproved a recent Alaska Supreme Court ruling that the state had to provide spousal benefits to same-sex partners of government employees.

While Palin later signed legislation that enforced the decision, she said she would support a ballot initiative that would effectively overturn the court ruling by banning gay spouses from state benefits.

Palin has also expressed support for the teaching of alternatives to evolution in public schools. According to the *Anchorage Daily News*, in response to a question on teaching evolution versus religious theories during a 2006 gubernatorial debate, Palin said, "Teach both. You know, don't be afraid of information. Healthy debate is so important, and it's so valuable in our schools. I am a proponent of teaching both."

The Supreme Court has ruled against the teaching of creationism in public schools, and other federal courts have extended that to a ban on teaching "intelligent design," a newer theory that states life is so complex that it necessitates the existence of an intelligent creative force of some sort.

Palin later, according to the newspaper, modified her position on public schools' teaching such theories. "I don't think there should be a prohibition against debate if it comes up in class," she said. "It doesn't have to be part of the curriculum."

Note that the August 2006 article from the Anchorage Daily News that covered this gubernatorial debate says that the exact question the moderator asked of Palin on this subject was: "[S]hould public schools teach alternatives to evolution (such as creationism and intelligent design)[?]"

Anchorage Daily News Oct. 23, 2006 article:

Palin's parents say they are not political and don't know how she decided to turn her ambition and work ethic toward politics. Her Christian faith, they say, came from her mother, who took her children to area Bible churches as they were growing up (Sarah is the third of four siblings). They say her faith has been steady since high school, when she led the Fellowship of Christian Athletes, and grew stronger as she sought out believers in her college years.

Palin doesn't brandish her religion on the campaign trail, but that doesn't prevent others from doing so. After she was first elected mayor, her predecessor, John Stein, objected that a Valley cable TV program had hailed her as Wasilla's first "Christian mayor." In a column for the local newspaper, he named eight previous mayors and added that he, too, was a Christian...

On religious leaders endorsing political candidates:

(Anchorage Daily News of October 2006 Alaska gubernatorial debate)(via **Jeffrey Weiss**):

[The debate moderator asked:] Is it OK for religious leaders to endorse candidates . . . .[?]

[The moderator] asked how they would feel if they walked into a church and heard a minister or pastor endorse a candidate for governor.

(Note, the following are excerpts, not the candidates' full responses.) . . . .

PALIN: "A pastor, a priest, a rabbi, certainly they have the freedom to say whatever they want to say. And you know, thank the lord that we do have that freedom of speech. "Faith is very important to so many of us here in America, and I would never support any government effort to stifle our freedom of religion or freedom of expression or freedom of speech.

"You know, I would just caution maybe a pastor to be very careful if they're in front of a congregation and they decide to endorse one candidate over another. You know, there may be some frustration with that candidacy endorsement being made manifest by a few, fewer dollars in the offering plate, so I would just offer that bit of caution. (laughing.) "But, no, I'll tell you, freedom of speech is so precious and it's worth defending and of course freedom of religion and freedom of expression will be things that I will fight for."

In School:

http://mensnewsdaily.com/2008/08/29/alaska-governor-sarah-palin-backgrounder/

Palin was the point guard and captain for the Wasilla High School Warriors, in Wasilla, Alaska, when they won the Alaska small-school basketball championship in 1982; she earned the nickname "Sarah Barracuda" because of her intense play. She played the championship game despite a stress fracture in her ankle, hitting a critical free throw in the last seconds. Palin, who was also the head of the school Fellowship of Christian Athletes, would lead the team in prayer before games.

In Politics:

http://www.christianpost.com/article/20080830/mccain-s-vp-choice-reassures-evangelicals.htm

As a politician, Palin has sided with the majority evangelical view in opposing gay marriage and expressing a desire to see creationism discussed alongside evolution in schools.

Creationism in public schools:

PALIN: "Teach both. You know, don't be afraid of information. "Healthy debate is so important and it's so valuable in our schools. I am a proponent of teaching both.

"And, you know, I say this, too, as the daughter of a science teacher. Growing up with being so privileged and blessed to be given a lot of information on, on both sides of the subject -- creationism and evolution.

"It's been a healthy foundation for me. But don't be afraid of information and let kids debate both sides."

On the war:

Palin from June 8, 2008 (via wasillaag.net):

Speaking before the Pentecostal church, Palin painted the current war in Iraq as a messianic affair in which the United States could act out the will of the Lord.

"Pray for our military men and women who are striving to do what is right. Also, for this country, that our leaders, our national leaders, are sending [U.S. soldiers] out on a task that is from God," she exhorted the congregants. "That's what we have to make sure that we're praying for, that there is a plan and that that plan is God's plan."

Religion, however, was not strictly a thread in Palin's foreign policy. It was part of her energy proposals as well. Just prior to discussing Iraq, Alaska's governor asked the audience to pray for another matter -- a $30 billion national gas pipeline project that she wanted built in the state. "I think God's will has to be done in unifying people and companies to get that gas line built, so pray for that," she said.

1306172